"Anger does not have to destroy marriage. As we encounter anger, we have a choice. Our choice is between the way of bitterness – which cancels out intimacy and leaves us isolated and alone; and the way of forgiveness – which opens the door to intimacy and love."

All too often anger robs married couples of the joy and satisfaction they long for in marriage. In *Refresh Your Marriage With Self Talk,* Dr. David Stoop and Jan Stoop explain that the key to refreshing a marriage is to resolve anger. By applying the principles of *self talk,* you can work out differences and diffuse anger with understanding and forgiveness. You'll learn how to open up lines of communication with your spouse and create rich and exciting changes, challenges, and rewards in your marriage.

BY David Stoop
Self-Talk: Key to Personal Growth

Dr. David Stoop & Jan Stoop

Refresh Your Marriage With Self Talk

Power Books

Fleming H. Revell Company
Old Tappan, New Jersey 07675

Scripture quotations not otherwise identified are from the Revised Standard Version of the Bible, copyrighted 1946, 1952, © 1971, and 1973.

Scripture quotations identified PHILLIPS are from LETTERS TO YOUNG CHURCHES by J. B. Phillips. Copyright © 1947, 1957 by Macmillan Publishing Co., Inc., renewed 1975 by J. B. Phillips. Used by permission.

Scripture quotations marked TLB are taken from The Living Bible, copyright 1971 by Tyndale House Publishers, Wheaton, IL. Used by permission.

Library of Congress Cataloging in Publication Data

Stoop, David A.
   Refresh your marriage with self-talk.

   "Power books."
   1. Marriage.   2. Anger.   3. Communication in marriage.
4. Forgiveness.   5. Marriage—Religious aspects—Christianity.   I. Stoop, Jan.   II. Title.
HQ734.S886   1984   646.7′8   84-8393
ISBN 0-8007-5164-7 (pbk.)

TO Mike and Lisa

Contents

Preface

Someone once said that if it weren't for marriage, husbands and wives would have to fight with strangers. Although it was meant as a joke, the statement is all too accurate in its portrayal of what marriage relationships often become. Too many marriages are locked into a pattern of continual conflict. If the struggle isn't obvious to the couple, or to an outside observer, it may simply mean that they have settled into a quiet, yet tense, truce, and the vitality of a loving relationship is missing.

This is a book about marriage—because we believe in marriage. It is also a book about anger—because we believe that difficulties in understanding anger make it the unidentified enemy that eats away at the joy and satisfaction we all long for in marriage. The key to REFRESHING a marriage—to putting the vitality and intimacy back into a relationship—is to resolve the issue of anger.

Through Dave's experience as a psychologist and marriage counselor, we have found that the most effective way to deal with emotions, and with anger in particular, is to teach people how to change the way they think—to change their Self-Talk. The course of a marriage is determined by our thoughts! The reason is that words have power, whether they are expressed through our mouth or spoken only in the privacy of our mind. As we explained in greater detail in the book *Self-Talk: Key to Personal Growth,* our thoughts determine the emotions we feel and the way we behave. Everyone uses Self-Talk, for each of us talks to himself. But it is *what* we are saying that determines the results.

Self-Talk goes far beyond the rather simplistic idea of "mind over matter." Its principles are based on a new theory of counseling known as cognitive therapy. But its roots go even deeper, for it is based on principles found in the Bible. Proverbs tell us that "as a man thinks in his heart, so is he" (*see* 23:7). Saint Paul wrote that we are to ". . . be transformed by the renewal of your mind" (Romans 12:2). He told us how to renew our minds when he wrote, ". . . take every thought captive to obey Christ" (2 Corinthians 10:5). The key to change is located within our thoughts.

You *can* create REFRESHING changes in your marriage. The way you can do it is to gain control of your emotions by gaining control of your thoughts. We get excited every time we see a couple put these principles to work in their marriage. Their success confronts us again with the fact that there is hope in any relationship when both people are willing to make an effort. We are indebted to these couples, for many of the ideas in this book were worked out in the time we have shared together in therapy. They have enriched our lives and our marriage by allowing us to share in the process of refreshing their marriage.

The principles in this book come not only from Dave's years as a counselor, but have also been worked out in the testing ground of our own marriage over the past twenty-seven years. The process of writing a book together forces us to draw even more heavily upon these same principles. *We* know they can work—our hope is that they will work in *your* marriage.

DAVE AND JAN STOOP

Refresh Your Marriage
With Self Talk

The land of marriage has this peculiarity, that strangers are desirous of inhabiting it, whilst its natural inhabitants would willingly be banished from thence.

MONTAIGNE

1

Cracks in the Wedding Bell

They sat on opposite ends of the couch, each one leaning away from the other. They were as far away from each other as they could get, and still be sitting on the same couch. They were describing what was left of their marriage with a strange sense of detachment, almost as if they were talking about the marriage of some distant relative.

Their situation was confusing, for I was getting mixed messages from both of them. They were coming for counseling, but neither one of them seemed to have any emotional investment in the marriage. In trying to evoke some response from them, I finally asked, "Why on earth do you want to stay married?" I wasn't prepared for their answer. One of them said, *"Every* other couple on our street is in the middle of a divorce, and we're trying to find some reason to stay together because *we don't want to be like every-*

one else." How sad, I thought to myself. I had never encountered such a fragile foundation upon which to rebuild
a marriage—but at least it was a starting point.

Marriage is under attack. Every day the media tells us in
one way or another that traditional marriage and the family are in trouble. The divorce rate has been climbing with
increasing velocity. Books and magazine articles extol the
joys of the various alternatives to the traditional marriage.
People proudly display on their license-plate holders their
belief that "happiness is being single." More couples are
coming to therapy today, but they come more with a sense
of ambivalence about their marriage than with a commitment to find ways to make it work.

Yet in the face of all this pressure on marriage, over 90
percent of us will marry in our lifetime. And while over a
third of all marriages will end in divorce, over 80 percent
of those divorced will remarry within three years. It's clear
that marriage is not suffering from a lack of popularity.
The problem appears to be one of making marriage work
better.

Over the years, the percentages of people getting married each year have remained essentially constant, but as
we are often told, the number of divorces has been increasing. During the last couple of years, the rate has slowed
down, but many researchers fear the slowdown is only a
reflection of the slowdown in the economy. It may be that
people cannot afford to get divorced right now. Only time
will tell whether this is true, or whether the rate has hit a
peak.

Researchers R. C. Glick and A. J. Norton present these statistics in another way. If you were married in 1950, one-fourth of the couples married that year with you would not have reached their twenty-fifth anniversary. They would be divorced. Among couples married in 1952, one-fourth would have been divorced by their twentieth anniversary. One-fourth of the couples married in 1958 did not make it to their fifteenth anniversary. And for couples married in 1965, one-fourth of them did not make it to their tenth anniversary. The statistics paint a dreary picture.

Anthropologist Margaret Mead cynically predicted the current situation when she wrote in 1949, "The American marriage ideal is one of the most conspicuous examples of our insistence on hitching our wagons to a star. It is one of the most difficult marriage forms that the human race has ever attempted."

What is it that makes our style of marriage so difficult? Why is divorce increasing at such an alarming rate? The answers to these questions can be as varied as the number of respondents.

Some would answer the questions by pointing to what they call our "naive expectations" about marriage. Couples enter marriage expecting that everything will work out. They expect that their marriage will last. Very quickly, they expect to become co-workers, co-parents, co-providers, lovers, and best friends. They naively expect these things to "just happen." And when one or more of these things don't happen, they walk away from the marriage.

Our grandparents did not place these demands on their

marriage. Maybe that's why their marriage lasted. For example, if we could go back in time some fifty years or so, and could interview the typical "happily married couple," we might get a response like this. He might say: "Of course I'm happy with my marriage. I've got a good wife. She's a hard worker—she makes sure there are three meals on the table every day. She sews, cleans, and keeps the clothes washed. And she's a good mother to the kids. What more could you ask for?"

His wife might say something like this: "Yes, I'm happy with my marriage. I've got a good husband. He works hard and comes home every night. And every Friday he brings home his paycheck. He's a good provider—he takes good care of me and the kids." If we asked her if her husband was her best friend, she might look puzzled, and then say, "Not really. He has a few good friends that he works with and he's still close to his brother. But whoever said your husband should be your best friend?" That marital goal was unheard of back then. If it happened, it was unexpected. Not so anymore!

Sociologists can look back over the past forty years and describe a new marital phenomenon—the "companionship marriage." We still want what our grandparents wanted, but we also want more. We want companionship and friendship from our spouse. And there is nothing wrong with that! It does, however, place an added burden on marriage. Those who feel we are naive in expecting our spouse to be our best friend say that this is one of the reasons for the rapid increase in the divorce rate.

Others, in an attempt to support the idea of companionship marriage take a different tack. They say it is naive for us to expect that two people can stay in love with the same person over a lifetime. They feed the current belief that when you "fall in love" with someone, you should get married, and when you "fall out of love" with that person, you should get a divorce. To them expecting that you can stay in love with the same person is an unrealistic expectation. So spouses come and go, just as friends come and go.

In counseling with couples, we see a large number of them caught in one or the other of these faulty ideas. Some come in complaining that they no longer "love" each other, but claim that they are still good friends. As a result, they are ambivalent about what to do. They get along okay, but can't find the passion anymore. They feel like roommates or like brother and sister. They had reached one part of the goal of a companionship marriage, but not the other. So they contemplate divorce as the solution.

Other couples come in to counseling frustrated because they have all the passion they want, but they can't get along with each other. They are lovers, but not friends. Often these couples have separated, only to move back together and find the cycle repeating itself. They can't live with each other, and they can't live without each other. So they too contemplate becoming part of the divorce statistics.

The problem here is not due to the expectations of the companionship marriage. There is nothing wrong with wanting your spouse to be your lover and friend. So even though our expectations for marriage have changed, that change alone does not account for the rise in the divorce rate. Other reasons are not hard to find. Ask anyone on the street why people get divorced and you'll come up with a list of reasons that would probably include the following: money problems, children problems, trouble with relatives, in-law problems, inability to communicate, sexual-adjustment problems, differences in temperament, just plain drifted apart, one partner fell in love with someone else, husband worked too much, interests were too different.

You could probably add a few more items to the list. And they would all seem valid. But, most of the obvious problems that lead couples to seek help, or lead to divorce, are "little" problems. Many couples coming to counseling admit to being embarrassed about what they are upset over in their marriage. "It seems like such a little thing when I say it," they protest. Yet it is these little things that grow to the point of becoming intolerable and appear to be unresolvable. Divorce often becomes the end result.

Tom came to my office by himself. He was a successful computer programmer who had been married for fifteen years. Two weeks earlier he had moved out of the house into his own apartment. Marge, his wife, was extremely distraught and Tom was concerned about her stability. Tom appeared to be a very quiet, reflective person, and he finally admitted that because of his quietness, his wife had no idea that for the past three years he was contemplating this move. The only reason he hadn't moved out earlier, according to Tom, was his concern about the reaction of his eleven-year-old daughter, Robin. When I pressed him for reasons why he had finally moved out, all he could say was, "I reached the end of my rope—we're just too different." For several sessions the answer was the same, "We're just too different—we're interested in different things." That was as specific as he could get.

Finally Tom agreed to let Marge come in with him, because he was still concerned that she be a good mother for Robin. Marge confirmed the fact that Tom's decision came "out of the blue." She could not understand his behavior but agreed that they were different. She noted, "It's only that he's quiet, and I've adjusted to that." No matter which way we approached the problem, Tom could only shrug his shoulders and repeat, "We're just too different, that's all." They are right. Here are two people who are very different.

Larry and Pam's problem was another matter. They were very much alike and anything but quiet. Larry was an expressive person, very content in his job as a sales manager. Pam was a very competent nurse and enjoyed the constant activity of working in the emergency room at the hospital. They were both very talkative. But for years they talked but never really heard each other. They had tried for years to learn how to communicate, but every workshop and seminar they attended only made things more tense.

With tears rolling down her face, Pam told of the times she had shared her deepest feelings with Larry. She said that even though he tried to understand, he always found something in what she was saying that he felt compelled to correct. He felt that he needed to explain how she had distorted some minor point. Even as Pam was explaining this, Larry jumped in to correct something she said. Later, as Larry was talking, I noticed that Pam did the same thing. They had a lot of knowledge about communication. They knew all the principles, but for years they were unable to hear each other. They are right. They have a communication problem.

John and Clare had argued about money even before they were married. John liked to spend it and Clare liked to save it. But on a teacher's salary there is not much to spend and even less to save. Clare said that she was the realist, and it was obvious that her main goal was to get John to sit down and face the limitations of their income. John agreed that there were limits, but accused Clare of being so shortsighted that if anything cost money she would purposely spoil it for him.

The problem took on a new dimension when Clare inherited a rather large sum of money. John figured that the pressure was off, but Clare stashed the money in a savings account and would not let John touch "her" money. She was afraid of his irresponsible attitudes about spending. For years they had fought about money because there was never enough. Now there appears to be enough, but the battle lines are redrawn and the war *rages* on. They are right. They have a problem about money.

Sarah and Chuck's problems seem to go along with success in the corporate world. Sarah occasionally longed for the days before he was so successful, but then would remember that even then he put in long hours in order to get ahead in business. Chuck readily admitted that he was a workaholic but would quickly remind Sarah that the trips she enjoyed, the jewelry she was wearing, the beautiful home she lived in, and the expensive car she drove were evidence of his commitment to her and the family. But as far as Sarah was concerned, she felt she would be happier living in a cottage and riding the bus if it meant she could have some time with Chuck.

Sarah talked about her loneliness, and as she shared those feelings, Chuck agreed that she was alone most of the time. But then he would point to the quality time they shared when on vacation. It was obvious that Chuck loved his work. He would get very animated and excited as he related things going on at the office. It was also obvious that he loved Sarah and the kids. But years ago he had made a choice to invest the greater portion of his time into his work. They are right. They have a problem with his work.

Each of these marriages has a different problem. And each problem is very real, causing a lot of pain and hurt. Unfortunately, our natural tendency when faced with these kinds of problems in a relationship is to feel that if we would only try a little harder, we could find a solution to the problem. Go back to Marge. She'll tell you how hard she's been trying to become what Tom wants her to be. Ever since he first commented on how different they are, she's been trying hard to develop areas that they can share.

But every time she finds something they could enjoy together, Tom finds something about it that will reinforce his belief that he and Marge are just "too different."

There's no question that Larry and Pam have been trying to solve their problem. They've been to counseling, retreats, courses at the community college, but nothing works. It seems the harder they try, the worse it gets.

Who should try harder in John and Clare's situation? They certainly want to solve their problem. Should Clare loosen up her attitudes toward money, or should John become more interested in saving money? John related that recently he had attended a workshop on investments, in an attempt to be more responsible. But that backfired, for Clare had no intention of letting him invest "her" money in some crazy scheme.

In a separate session, Chuck admitted that he'd quit trying to please Sarah. He attempted in the past, but it seemed that the harder he tried to do what Sarah wanted, the more she wanted from him. Since he figured he could never do enough, he decided to dig in his heels and enjoy his work.

Trying harder to resolve a problem seems like a very reasonable thing to do. Unfortunately, our attempts to try harder only serve to prove the truth of the principle that TRYING HARDER ONLY GETS YOU MORE OF THE SAME. We can be shown situations that prove the truth of that principle, yet we continue to try harder and harder, and end up with more of the same problem.

Does that mean that "trying harder" is the real culprit behind the problems in marriage? Not really. It's only another complicating factor that comes from focusing on the obvious difficulties and not digging deeper for the real problem. It's easy to blame the obvious problems. But to get to the root of the matter, we need to resist the obvious and look further. That's where we'll find the real cause of marital discord.

QUESTIONS TO CONSIDER:

1. Make a list of all the things you like about your husband/wife. After you make the list, set a time and share your lists with each other.
2. Imagine yourselves five years in the future. Together you have worked out all the snags in your relationship. You have the "ideal" marriage—everything you ever dreamed about. On a separate sheet of paper write down all the things that make your marriage so satisfying. Then set a time when you can share your lists with each other.

The irony of anger is that it never works in changing others.

WAYNE DYER

2

The Problem Behind the Problems

Several years ago the *Journal of Marriage and Family Counseling* featured an article in which the author rather tentatively suggested that "what causes marriages to fail, over and over again, is the incapacity of the couple to cope with their own and each other's anger." In his recent book *Love and Anger in Marriage*, that same author, David Mace, has expanded his ideas and asserts that marriage generates in normal people more anger than they will encounter in any other relationship. Our inability to effectively process and communicate this anger lies at the root of marital discord and divorce.

Why have we overlooked the problems of anger in marriage for so long? Perhaps it's because anger can take so many forms. It can be witty or just plain catty; it can take the form of a clever remark or a verbal sock in the stomach. It can be an exploding temper, or glaring silence. Some forms of anger seem childish, so as adults we discover more subtle and clever ways of expressing anger.

Many of us are very angry but almost totally unaware of it. Others are angry and know it, but feel trapped because they don't know how to get rid of those feelings. We try to pretend we have no anger, but there is chaos within. A major internal riot threatens to erupt at the slightest provocation.

Many of us are confused about anger, because somewhere along the way we were taught that anger should not exist in our lives. We need to be reassured that anger is a perfectly valid and natural human emotion. Husbands and wives let each other down; they say things they don't mean; they forget to do something they promised to do; they get their priorities turned around. When these things happen, we will feel anger. It is a way of saying, "Notice my needs!" When something happens that does not affirm our worth as humans, we are prone to get angry. It's part of our emotional makeup, placed there by God.

"But," some of you protest, "I don't ever get angry!" If you feel that way, be assured that our intention is not to turn you into an angry person. However, if anger is a valid human emotion, and you say you don't ever get angry, then you are missing out on part of life. For some, our religious training has prompted us to deny the existence of anger. "Righteous indignation" was acceptable for Jesus, and perhaps for us in *extreme* situations—but not anger! So for those of you who never get "angry" it will help you understand what we are saying in this chapter as well as in the rest of this book, if you simply erase the word *anger*, and substitute a word like *annoyance, frustration*, or *irritation*. The principles will be the same.

I think the one person who experienced an intense struggle with anger—perhaps even more than we do—was the Apostle Paul. He wrestled with anger because he was basically an angry man.

When we first meet him, he is called Saul. He is enraged at the new religion, at the Christians. Perhaps a fellow Jew might have said that Paul was righteously indignant, but in reality, Paul was extremely angry.

Later on, when Saul became Paul and experienced the new birth, he was faced with the consequences of his anger. He had vivid memories of times when he lost control, and his anger exploded. So as he wrote to the young Christian churches, he warned them over and over of the dangers associated with anger. He wrote to the Colossians, telling them to "put them all away: anger, wrath, malice, slander, and foul talk from your mouth" (Colossians 3:8).

Probably the best insight into Paul's struggle with anger is seen in his letter to the Galatians. Notice where he lists anger: "Now the works of the flesh are plain: [immorality], impurity, licentiousness, idolatry, sorcery, enmity, strife, jealousy, anger, selfishness, dissension, party spirit, envy, drunkenness, carousing, and the like" (Galatians 5:19–21). Get rid of your anger, Paul admonishes. Note that everything else on his list is either a behavior or an attitude; anger is the only emotion listed. And everything on the list is to be eliminated from our life.

Part of Paul's struggle with the emotion of anger is due to the fact he was a very devout Jew, a Pharisee. He knew the Old Testament well. Perhaps later, when he visited the Church in Galatia, one of the new Christians who had also been a Pharisee came up to him and reminded him about the number of times the word *anger* is used in the Old Testament. "Paul," he might have said, "Remember the rabbi who had us count words in the Old Testament? Remember how many times the word *anger* was used?" And Paul would nod his head in agreement, knowing that the word *anger* is used over 450 times in the Old Testament.

Then his friend would add, "Paul, how can you say that anger is a sin, when over 75 percent of those references relate to God's anger?" And Paul knew that most of the other references involved the anger of the great men of faith.

Paul struggled deeply with that issue. His struggle was complicated by his knowledge of Jesus' anger. Jesus showed anger a number of times. For example, in Mark 3, His anger is very clear:

> Again he entered the synagogue, and a man was there who had a withered hand. And they watched him, to see whether he would heal him on the sabbath, so that they might accuse him. And he said to the man who had the withered hand, "Come here." And he said to them, "Is it lawful on the sabbath to

do good or to do harm, to save life or to kill?" But they were silent. *And he looked around at them with anger,* grieved at their hardness of heart, and said to the man, "Stretch out your hand." He stretched it out, and his hand was restored.

MARK 3:1–6 (italics added)

How did Paul reconcile his concerns about anger with these examples? How could he say that anger is the work of the flesh—sin? If God's anger punctuates the Old Testament, and Jesus obviously experienced anger at times, what was Paul going to do with his fears that anger could be so evil?

Use your imagination to picture how Paul might have stewed over this dilemma. He is in prison and is busy writing a letter to the Ephesian Christians. Perhaps something happened during the day that made Paul very angry. All of the struggles with his anger come to the surface of his mind, and as he attempts to sleep, he tosses and turns fitfully. Suddenly, he sits up, wide awake.

"I've got it!" he shouts, waking everyone up, including his scribe, Tychicus. Paul is excited. He asks Tychicus to write something down. "I've got another thought I want in that letter we were writing." And he tells Tychicus to write, "Be angry but do not sin!" Sometimes I imagine that Paul quickly falls asleep, while his scribe is awake the rest of the night trying to figure out what Paul meant.

One almost wants to join Tychicus and wake Paul up demanding, "What do you mean by that?" I think one of the first times I read that verse I thought to myself, *That feels so good! Now I can get angry.* But then I wondered how I could get angry and not sin. Of course, when I became angry, I didn't worry about the "not sinning" part. All I knew was that it felt good to be angry, at least at the time.

It's only afterward that we begin to feel bad about what we said or did in our anger. That's why we get stuck in the same struggle as Paul. Anger feels good for it is a valid human emotion. But the results of our anger throw us into the same kind of confusion Paul must have experienced. And when anger invades our marriage, as it inevitably does, the struggle is intensified, for in our most intimate relationships, we simply do not know how to communicate effectively to the other person what we are angry about.

Let's look again at the couples we met in the first chapter and see how unresolved anger is the current that runs just beneath the surface. Tom's silence and then his aggressive action in moving out of the house are both expressions of anger. In fact, if you were to meet Tom, you would be able to sense his anger, as I did. But when I asked him about his anger, he said he was completely unaware of any such feelings. Nonetheless, the way he controlled his emotions gave the impression that if he experienced one little show of emotion, it would let loose an explosion that would destroy the whole neighborhood. It appeared that even his moving out of the house was done in order to keep his anger under complete control.

Marge's anger is just beginning to come to the surface.

For years she had redirected her anger by cleaning the house, polishing the silver, taking care of the kids, or just by trying harder to be the model wife Tom desired. In between she struggled a lot with feelings of depression, but cleaning out a closet usually helped. Since Tom has moved out, she's aware of feelings she has held in for years. In fact, they both agreed that not an angry word had been expressed by either of them until Tom moved out.

For fifteen years they had not one argument, or even a cross word between them. Now you only hear angry words from Marge—Tom is acting his anger out through his behavior. And without some help, their anger will destroy whatever is left of their marriage.

Larry and Pam don't like the word *anger*. If you press the issue, they will agree that they are frustrated, irritated, and even deeply bothered—but never really angry. Larry's parents were a good example of angry people. They fought all the time. He can remember lying in his bed with his pillow over his head to block out the sounds of their violent arguments.

Pam's parents were just the opposite of Larry's. She does not remember ever hearing them raise their voices at each other or at the kids. She can remember sermons she heard in her church about anger's being sinful. Discussions at Sunday dinner following those sermons added to the deep impression made on a young girl. They both had good reasons to avoid the word *anger*.

But remember, the word you use for anger isn't important. The emotion you feel and the process you experience remain the same. Pam and Larry's problem in communication is the obvious problem—anger lies beneath the surface. Watch them as they try so hard. Pam wants to "discuss" something and Larry is willing to make the effort. But as soon as Pam gets too involved in the details, Larry clams up. Pam then tries a little harder to make her point, being careful not to raise her voice, until finally Larry jumps back into the discussion in self-defense. As he defends himself by carefully explaining his side of the issue, she gets defensive and has to go into a more detailed argument defending her side of the issue.

Depending on their energy level and the time of day when the "discussion" started, their explanations will see-saw back and forth until one of them either gives up or withdraws in frustration. Both feel irritation and hurt—both synonyms for anger.

John and Clare are very open about their anger. They always have been. For years Clare has been very outspoken in her criticism of John. He's never been willing to consider becoming a principal, much to Clare's distress. He's not even been willing to take graduate courses to improve his pay scale. Both of these issues were examples to Clare of his irresponsible attitude toward their financial security. Everyone knows Clare's feelings on these matters. If they don't, she will be happy to fill them in.

When Clare received her inheritance, John became much more vocal about his anger. He's very critical of Clare's independence, her Scrooge-like attitude toward him, and her total disregard for how hard he has worked. It used to be that Clare started the arguments, but now John is the initiator. Their anger spills out all over the place. Before it was uncomfortable; now it is frightening.

Sarah has become very open about her anger at Chuck. In fact, she threatened him with divorce if he didn't agree to counseling. She's very quick to point out his shortcomings: He doesn't understand her emotional needs; he isn't sensitive; he's too logical and unfeeling; he has ice in his veins; he doesn't even know how to love someone.

Chuck seems to let her anger simply roll off him, but a funny little remark here, or a humorous quip there, and Sarah quickly gets the point. His humor used to be funny, but lately it's been sharp and cutting. Sometimes you can see Sarah literally wince from the pain.

In each of these situations, the obvious problems eventually took a backseat as anger emerged and took center stage. But we must be careful not to let anger be the culprit, for as we have already pointed out, anger is a valid and necessary human emotion. Whenever there are problems, there will be anger. Anger may be at the root of the problem, but the real culprit in marriage is our inability to effectively and creatively process and communicate that anger.

Perhaps an illustration will help. If you are driving along the highway and someone cuts in front of you as though he never saw you, you would probably get angry. But if, when you leaned on your horn, that person looked in his rearview mirror and then waved an apology, your anger would quickly fade. Why? Because you would feel that you had effectively communicated your anger by honking your horn and the other person had courteously acknowledged his error with a waved apology.

The same is true with anger in marriage. The problem is not that we get angry—that is inevitable. The trouble is that we so seldom ever get an acknowledgment from the other person that indicates he understands what we are feeling. We don't know how to communicate our feelings of anger in a way that allows us to be heard. And even if we hear the anger in our spouse, we don't know how to respond except with anger and defensiveness of our own.

If we get angry in any other relationship, we can leave it. Even if our anger is directed at our parents, we can leave home, or cut off contact with them. But the situation in a marriage is different. Leaving is much more complex in that our whole purpose in getting married is to find understanding and to experience mutual affection and intimacy. So we stay, and get in trouble with our anger.

We also get in trouble with our anger at home because it is easy to forget the rules that our culture has set up to help us control our anger. Without rules regarding anger, we would soon be living in anarchy. But anarchy sometimes reigns within the home because couples forget to follow the rules of courtesy when they are angry. Most violence in our society takes place within the family. It appears that it is easier to follow the rules of courtesy with strangers than with the one we love the most.

The problems couples have with anger have been compounded by well-meaning counselors who advise us to vent our anger. Too many marriages have collapsed under the weight of ventilated anger. Our culture tends to encourage emotional expression, regardless of the hurt and damage it may cause. It almost seems as if our task in marriage is to conquer the other person by intimidating them with our anger. Perhaps it is a result of our individualism. But every time we place the desires of self at the top of the list, anger will not be far behind. Ventilating our anger in marriage is not the answer, regardless of who is suggesting it.

A survey taken several years ago supports what we are saying in this chapter. Couples who reported that they were happy in their marriage did not have any fewer problems and conflicts than unhappy couples. Nor did they feel any less angry. The only difference the researchers could identify was that happy couples had found a way to process their anger. Their experience shows us that anger and love can coexist. They have to, for people rarely feel much anger with people they don't care about.

QUESTIONS TO CONSIDER:

1. What are some of the areas in your marriage in which you have been able to talk through your anger?
2. What made it possible for you to communicate effectively your feelings of anger in the above areas?
3. Where do you need further help in communicating your anger?

Therefore a man leaves his father and his mother and cleaves to his wife, and they become one flesh.

GENESIS 2:24

3

Can Two Really Become One?

The relationship between love and anger is confusing, partly because we so often equate anger with hate. In our anger at someone, we can often be heard to mutter under our breath, "Oh, how I *hate* that person!"

I often ask people in counseling, or in a seminar, "What is the opposite of love? The answer given almost every time is "hate." Since we usually tie anger and hate together in our thinking, it is easy to come to the conclusion that the opposite of love is anger.

The truth is that neither anger nor hate are the opposite of love. The opposite of love is fear. We see this in the Bible when John writes that "There is no fear in love, but perfect love casts out fear" (1 John 4:18). One dispels the other, for they are opposite emotions. But unlike love and fear, love and anger are not incompatible. In reality, the more we love, the more potential we have for anger. We can only get angry if there is something there that we care about.

To better understand how love and anger relate, we need to look at how our emotions work. Most psychologists agree that humans experience three basic emotions—love, fear, and anger. From these core emotions radiate the myriad range of feelings.

All three of these emotions are normal experiences for each of us. Love is usually seen as a positive emotion, for its results are usually positive. We often hear people define anger and fear as negative emotions, but they have positive aspects: For if we didn't feel anger or fear at times, we would place ourselves in life-threatening situations. Being angry or being afraid can sometimes save our lives.

We usually think of anger and fear as negative emotions because most of our experiences with anger and fear have been negative. We are afraid, and so we avoid an experience that will benefit us. Or we express our anger and the situation gets worse because we are angry.

Perhaps it would help us if we could see that the *initial* experience of either anger or fear is a neutral warning device built into our systems. The problem comes with what we do after that initial experience of fear or anger. If we hang on to our anger and nurse it into rage or bitterness or vengeance, we will have a negative experience. If we get trapped in our fears, we can become overly anxious, or even phobic. The negative aspects of these two emotions are associated not with the emotion itself, but with the way we process these emotions.

Another way to understand the three basic emotions is to look at the movement attached to each emotion. The movement of love is *toward* the person or object of our love. The movement of fear is *away* from the person or object of our fear. The movement of anger is *against* the person or object of our anger. As you consider the movement of the emotions, you can easily see that the movement of love and of fear are opposite movements—*away* from and *toward*. Love and fear are opposite emotions. The movement of love and of anger are in the same direction—*toward* or *against*—only the intensity and intent are different.

Let's look at how these emotions operate with a typical couple. As our couple moves toward marriage, they are in love not only with each other, but with the idea of marriage itself. They spend a lot of time moving closer to each other. When they can't be together, they talk on the phone or write letters to each other. Everything they do is defined as movement *toward* each other. During this time they overlook a number of little things that could cause problems. They want nothing to interfere with the building of their love—their movement *toward* each other.

Sometimes couples move too fast, and become afraid. That's when they pull back in fear, moving *away* from each other. But then their love takes over and they begin to move *toward* each other again.

But sometime after the wedding the honeymoon ends. Something changes. Those little things that didn't matter so much before gradually begin to interfere with the movement of love. The patient tolerance expressed before the marriage no longer operates as effectively in the face of irritants. The couple finds that the road gets a little rocky. They may even experience some angry outbursts. What can they do? They want love, closeness, mutual affection, understanding, companionship, intimacy—not anger. In order to reach these goals, they must continue to move closer together. But they are stymied. In their desire to reach all those positive, warm, and loving objectives, they find themselves experiencing anger instead.

In an effort to break through the impasse, our couple makes a renewed commitment and begins to move *toward* each other. But the harder they try, the more difficult the task becomes. A flood of horrible questions and feelings begins to well up inside each of them. Did they marry the right person? Is this what other couples experience? Why are they beginning to feel so much hostility, resentment, anger, and fear? What are they to do? If they continue to push toward their goal of intimacy, the tension and pressure they feel makes it a movement *against* the other person. They will experience more anger. Should they pull back in fear and begin to move *away* from the object of their love? That may feel better inside, but it is a contradictory movement and usually brings with it feelings of confusion and disillusionment.

So our couple is in a real quandary. If they continue to press toward their goal of love and intimacy, the anger they feel threatens to consume their love. On the other hand, if they pull back and move away from each other, they will be giving up the very goals that brought them together in the first place.

Often, couples go through this love-anger-fear cycle a number of times, eventually finding their love has burned out or is a mere flicker of their early dreams and desires. When they realize this, they sometimes settle for a position of compromise in which they experience little love or intimacy. Erik Erickson has identified this hollow type of relationship in which very little love is experienced as *isolation à deux*—two people living isolated lives, even though they live in the same house. We might picture this kind of relationship as being like two people, each living inside a glass vacuum tube, occasionally bumping into each other. But only the sound of the clanking glass is heard. The two people no longer ever really "touch" each other.

Other couples settle for what looks like a ritual dance. The husband and wife are connected, but what connects them is a twenty-foot pole. Each person is attached to one end of the pole. As the wife begins to move *toward* her husband, he backs *away*. He has no choice, really, for the pole pushes him away. When the wife tires of trying to get closer, the husband begins to move *toward* his wife, in search of love and intimacy. But now the wife backs *away*, for she has to maintain the distance determined by the pole. Sometimes couples break the pole and find closeness, but usually the result is two people who settle for a life determined by a "pole." They become "distant lovers."

Why is it that in our search for love and intimacy we encounter so much anger? What makes us so afraid? Why do we tie ourselves to "poles" that keep us at a distance from the one we love? Why is it so hard to go beyond the anger and find intimacy?

There is no simple answer to these questions. But if we can look at the different attempts to find an answer, we might get some insight into how we get entangled in the love-anger-fear cycle. Let's look at four possible explanations.

1. Intimacy is threatening.

Closeness can be a very frightening and threatening experience. We are really afraid to be known by someone else, especially a spouse. Even though we want intimacy, we are unwilling to risk having someone know where we are weak, or where we feel most vulnerable. We long for closeness, but only if it is safe. And no one can guarantee it will be safe.

John Powell, in his book *Why Am I Afraid to Tell You Who I Am?* says that I am afraid "because, if I tell you who I am, you may not like who I am, and it's all that I have." We all carry within us what he calls "secrets." These are our past hopes, dreams, and shames, and they are uniquely a part of us. Even if we could put them into words, we could not be sure of how they would sound to our mate, and even less sure of what our mate would do with them. So we lock them away inside us. We want closeness, but we simply are afraid to take the risk.

2. Fear may be seen as weakness.

If we are afraid and threatened by intimacy, we may also think that others will perceive this fear as weakness. No one really wants to be seen as a weak person. It's one thing to be afraid; it's quite a different matter to appear weak.

In order to compensate for our supposed weaknesses, we grit our teeth and act tough. Husbands, in order to hide their fear of intimacy, put on a "macho" front to make sure people don't see them as being weak. Sometimes they actually set out to intimidate the one they love, just to prove this point. They are operating in the mistaken belief that if they can substitute anger for fear, they will appear to be strong. In the process, their anger eventually smothers any remaining feelings of love.

3. Intimacy equals dependency.

Closeness and intimacy with a spouse can also be seen as a form of dependency. We all want to be self-sufficient and we believe that dependency is at the opposite end of the scale. Spouses who are struggling with feelings of dependency try to eliminate those feelings by pulling away from their partner and set out to prove their independence. They are certain that if they don't pull away, they will become *too* much in love, or get *too* close, and end up being consumed by their partner and lose any sense of self-identity.

Anger is a way of responding to feelings of dependency. When we get angry, we are struggling to restore some degree of self-sufficiency. A certain degree of self-sufficiency is good, but the overcompensating search for total self-sufficiency is a barrier to intimacy. People who overemphasize self-sufficiency have a hard time experiencing love, and often end up as loners, even within their marriage.

4. Anger must be blocked.

Sometimes we think the solution to the love-anger-fear cycle is to eliminate the feelings of anger and fear. Then all we would be left with are the feelings of love, freeing us to move toward the goal of intimacy. What we overlook with this line of reasoning is that our attempts to block the emotions of anger and fear lead to a generalized blockage of all of our emotions. We cannot experience love, joy, happiness, and other positive feelings without experiencing the dark side of emotions and feelings. If we attempt to block one type of emotion, we end up blocking all of them. Perhaps that is why some couples seem to lose any sense of love in their relationship. Over the years, they have carefully blocked any awareness of the negative emotions, never realizing that at the same time they were inhibiting the flow of love.

The love-anger-fear cycle can be perpetuated by our inadequate definitions of love, as well as by our problems with anger and fear. When couples block their anger and fear, and end up blocking any sense of love as well, we call this "falling out of love." Unfortunately, our culture's definitions of love make it appear to be impossible to ever "fall back in love" again with the same person. Much of what we call "love" comes from the "Courts of Love," which were organized by the wives of the Crusaders back in the Middle Ages. These Courts defined the rules and traditions of "love," but for these lonely women, love was equated with extramarital passion. One of their "Codes of Love," dated in the twelfth century, included points such as these:

- Every lover turns pale at the sight of the co-lover.
- The lover's heart trembles at the unexpected sight of the co-lover.
- A new love makes one quit the old.
- If love lessens, it dies speedily and rarely regains health.
- Suspicion, and the jealousy it kindles, increase love's worth.

The summation of this code is as follows: "We pronounce and decree by the tenour of these presents, that love cannot extend its powers over two married persons."

These ideas marked the beginnings of what we call "romantic" love.

Over the centuries, these concepts have continued to color our understanding of love. The problem with these ideas about love is that the whole area of commitment is ignored. A definition of love that I found a number of years ago gives us a whole different perspective in which to view the emotion of love. Love is defined as, "an emotional-volitional response to an intellectual evaluation of another person." The emotions and the will make a *choice* to love based on an intelligent appraisal.

There are other good definitions of love, but the reason I like this one is that it places the emphasis on choice. We love because we *choose* to love. Therefore, we stop loving because we *choose* to stop loving. And if our love has simply faded away and died, it can be rekindled if we *choose* to love again.

Whenever couples say to me that they don't love their spouse anymore, or that they aren't sure, I always reply, "Oh, that's nothing to be concerned about, we don't have to worry about that issue." Then, in order to reduce their shock, I explain to them that it is amazing how love can grow again when we make a *choice* to love and begin to act in loving ways toward each other. The best way to stay in love is to choose to love.

QUESTIONS TO CONSIDER:

1. Think of times when you have experienced the "movement" of the emotions of love, anger, and fear. Describe what happened.
2. Can you think of situations when you have been caught in the love-fear-anger cycle?
3. Describe times when either you or your spouse have successfully worked through the problems of the love-fear-anger cycle and experienced intimacy.

Be angry but do not sin.
EPHESIANS 4:26

4

The Behaviors of Anger

The problem with anger is that we seldom know what to do with it. We search for solutions in books and seminars that promise to tell us how we can resolve our anger. The advice we find ranges from supposedly new and better ideas about how to ventilate our anger to rules and gimmicks that are designed to help us control our anger. The message is that our anger can be effectively channeled if we can only become a better ventilator or a better controller. Unfortunately, when we try to implement this advice, we discover that the new behaviors are as ineffective as the old ones in helping us resolve our anger. The problem remains. Anger still intrudes into our marriage, infects our family, and touches every other important relationship we have.

An interesting study with disturbing results was conducted by a team of psychologists several years ago. The stated intent of the study was to investigate family communication patterns around the dinner table. A researcher would visit each of the families that volunteered for the study, and set up a videotape machine to record the family's conversations during dinner. With each family, the procedure went something like this.

Just as the family was sitting down for dinner, the researcher "remembered" that he had a very important phone call to make and asked the family members to please excuse him for a short time. He then asked the individual family members to take turns and practice pointing the video camera at the rest of the family. He assured them that even the youngest family member could handle it, for everything else was automatic. He said he would start the tape over when he finished his phone call.

The phone call inevitably lasted throughout the entire dinner hour, for that was part of the researcher's plan. Just as with most psychological studies, the stated purpose of the study was not what the researchers were really investigating.

As dinner was ending, the researcher would return from his phone call with apologies for being held up so long. He assured the family that if what they had already done did not serve the purpose of the study, another taping would be scheduled. He explained that he had tried to resolve a matter over the phone but could not, so he had to return to the office. He thanked them for being so helpful in going ahead with things while he was tied up.

Later, when all the videotapes were examined, it was

found that, almost without exception, whoever was running the camera made an effort to focus on some negative behavior taking place around the table. It did not matter whether it was one of the parents or one of the kids who was operating the camera; their main desire seemed to be to show different members of the family in a bad light.

Now why would family members want to do that? What was their motivation? The researchers felt that the results of their study demonstrated that the primary emotion exhibited in family interaction was anger. The attempts to make other family members look bad was a subtle expression of unresolved anger. It appears that the search for closeness within a family produces the same angry response that we observe in the marriage relationship.

I see these unresolved feelings surfacing at times in my relationship with my own kids. When this happens, all I can see are the negative things—the things they don't do right. It doesn't matter what honors they receive, or what accomplishments they achieve, I still focus on the things they do not do right. In my desire to be close to them, I look for intimacy but find frustration instead. In picking at the negative aspects of their behavior, I end up pushing my sons away from me and lose the closeness that I am seeking. We all do it—in wanting intimacy, we force the opposite to take place. When we get close to someone, the negatives somehow seem to loom so large that they dominate our perception.

The behavior of anger comes in many different disguises. Couples usually settle into predictable patterns of angry behavior, but because anger is easily camouflaged, those particular behaviors may be difficult to identify. Here are some of the common ones.

1. Avoiding the crisis

We already described this behavior when we looked at Tom in the first chapter. This behavior represents a refusal to face even the possibility of a conflict. Even when the other partner tries to express feelings of hurt or anger, he gets nothing in response. The "avoider" may leave the room, or even leave the house. He is great at falling asleep while being talked to, or can get very busy with a book, a TV program, or some project in the garage or the sewing room. He will do anything to avoid dealing with the problem. His mate ends up feeling as though she is boxing with her own shadow.

The "avoider" is saying either that he is too afraid of his own angry feelings to stop and consider the crisis, or that he is too afraid of his partner's anger. In this situation, it sometimes helps to see that behind the anger is a tremendous amount of fear that will never respond to confrontation.

2. Tickling the crisis

This behavior is almost as indirect as that of avoidance. The person never really brings up what is bothering him;

he just tickles the problem and then backs away. For instance, the wife will not directly confront her concern about her husband's overcommitted schedule. Instead, she drops a little hint by innocently asking, "Oh, you have another meeting tonight?" If her husband picks up the bait, she quickly retreats by saying something like, "No, I just forgot. Go ahead, I'll take care of things here."

Inside, she is angry! She is willing to go one small step beyond the "avoider" and drop a hint about what is bothering her. But she stays away from dealing directly with the problem, hoping that if she tickles the problem often enough with subtle hints, her mate will eventually get the message and change his behavior.

3. Pouring on the guilt

This behavior goes a step beyond "tickling the crisis." Instead of tickling the issue, the person avoids the problem, but tries to change his mate through guilt. This person often takes *all* the blame for any problem that comes up. For example, as a way of avoiding the real issues of his wife's complaints about their relationship, the husband will say: "I know it's all my fault. I'm to blame for all of our problems. She's been so patient and understanding, and I've just blown it time after time. I don't know why she's put up with me."

The wife retreats, feeling guilty. What more can she say? If he is really good at pouring it on, he can reinforce her guilt by adding something like, "But it's okay. Don't worry about me (sigh)." The husband's use of guilt is a disguised way of saying to his wife, "I am angry with you, but I am not willing to tell you what it is about." He is afraid of what the consequences might be if he admits to being angry. Making her feel guilty keeps the focus away from himself.

4. Changing the subject

Couples like to use this behavior, especially in counseling situations. Changing the subject is almost an automatic response to any awareness of anger. The reason it works so well is that regardless of which partner initiates this behavior, the other person is willing to be distracted. Just as the discussion seems to be moving close to some very important issues, one partner will bring up some new subject, totally "out of the blue." And just as quickly, the discussion takes off in that new direction, with both people appearing relieved. Sometimes the other spouse is frustrated by this behavior but seems powerless in being able to get the discussion back on the original track. By following the new topic of conversation, both husband and wife are able to avoid any feelings of anger that they might be experiencing. What they are saying with this behavior is "We are getting too close to what I am angry about and I am not willing to expose it yet."

5. *Distracting with criticism*

This is another form of "changing the subject" and is a good example of the principle "the best defense is a good offense." Instead of dealing with the issue at hand, attention is diverted by an "out of the blue" critical statement. A husband might say, without any relevance at all to the discussion, "I wish you were more feminine." What wife can ignore that kind of statement? The basic form of the criticism is nonspecific. It not only leaves the other person speechless, but it also gives the criticizer time and room to maneuver.

This behavior usually represents a greater intensity of anger, and it is more destructive to the relationship. Often, couples save this one, using it only when they feel themselves being backed into a corner with no room for retreat. In the example, the husband is not willing to be specific about what he is angry about, so he hides his anger behind some vague accusation. The anger is felt by the receiver, but the criticizer can safely deny the existence of the anger.

6. *Accommodation*

This is probably the ultimate form of angry behavior designed to avoid the issues. The "accommodator" differs from the other avoiders because he is making an effort to avoid conflict by being too nice. This partner is not playing the martyr, the one pouring on the guilt, but is truly going out of his way to be nice, doing everything he or she can to please the other person—to avoid conflict through accommodation.

This is probably the most passive expression of anger we can use. It is a "peace at any price" type of behavior. The person using this type of angry behavior usually drives his partner "up the wall" and instead of eliminating conflict and problems, he or she increases the intensity of the anger in the relationship.

7. Setting the trap

This can be one of the most frustrating of the angry behaviors on our list. "Setting the trap" is an underhanded behavior, and in many cases it is very difficult to identify. The "trap" can be set so subtly that the "trapped" person never even knows what is happening. Eventually, though, they catch on and feel that they have been set up and become extremely hurt and angry.

The traps can be very simple or very complex. For example, a wife can set a trap by telling her husband how nice it would be if he would send her flowers once in a while. Finally, when her message sinks in, the husband sends her a beautiful flower arrangement. When he arrives home, expecting love and adoration for his thoughtfulness, he finds his wife preoccupied, almost as if she were giving him the cold shoulder. When he asks her if she liked the flowers, she says something like, "Yes, they were okay, but it is not the same when I have to ask for them." He was set up—by an angry wife.

8. Mind reading

Reading the partner's mind is a common behavior that is guaranteed to raise the level of anger in a relationship. The "mind reader" enjoys the luxury of never having to listen to what his mate is saying. Instead of listening, he interrupts by saying something like, "The *real* reason you feel that way is . . ." and then goes on to explain what the other person *really* means by what she is saying. Examples of endings to the above statement include, ". . . that you really don't like my mother," or ". . . that you really wish you had married Joe."

When spouses are really good at this, they can often get their partner to drop the original thought and become caught up in defending themselves against what the mind reader is saying. Sometimes they can get the other partner so confused that they don't really know what it was they were thinking or trying to say in the first place. Because it is an angry behavior, mind readers often feel their observation is valid, never realizing their anger distorted their perception.

9. Tyrannizing with the trivial

Because this is a more expressive form of angry behavior, it is usually a very reliable way to increase the anger of a spouse. It is often used as an angry behavior with the motivation of "getting even." This person actually does things that irritate, such as leaving a glass on the TV, belching at the dinner table, cracking gum, stealing the punch line of a story, or doing just about anything he or she knows is offensive to the other person.

This behavior often takes on a form in which one partner constantly interrupts the discussion in order to "help" the other person be more accurate. The interruptions focus on trivial points, which have little or no relevance to the discussion. Phrases like "You can't keep anything straight, it was . . ." or "Your memory is really lousy, I never . . ." or "You've got to get your facts straight, what really happened was . . ." are used to introduce the trivia. A good "trivia tyrant" can increase his mate's frustration level *and* divert the discussion at the same time, thus subtly disguising his own anger.

10. Placing the blame

This is a common angry behavior, almost as common as being part of the human race. *No one* really wants to take the blame for anything! This behavior is an angry form of defensiveness that seeks to put the blame on the other person. When couples begin to use "placing the blame," the whole point of the discussion shifts from the issues to finding out who is at fault. It is a finger-pointing behavior, and can heat up an already tense disagreement. There is seldom any question that this is an angry behavior on the part of both spouses.

What this behavior overlooks is that both partners are usually at fault—so both sides of the argument are right. Our perceptions of events are always somewhat distorted, for we see things from our own point of view. So if two people who have experienced something—each perceiving it from his own point of view, and both being right about what they perceived—begin to use "placing the blame," the result will surely be an increase in their anger.

11. Gunnysacking

Another name for this behavior is "collecting trading stamps." Instead of getting involved and facing the conflict, people turn to this behavior in an attempt to control their anger. While it appears that they have been calmly avoiding the issues, they have really been storing away all their feelings of anger, as though they were stuffing them into a gunnysack. When the sack is about to burst, they dump it out on some unsuspecting victim. It's almost as if they feel that since they have been saving up their "anger stamps," they can trade in their "stamp book" for a temper tantrum. Sometimes, "gunnysackers" will trade in their "stamp book" for an expensive shopping spree, a food or alcohol binge, or a trip home to mother. The person who uses this type of behavior gives the impression of starting with a clean slate after the sack is emptied, but this is not the case. In reality, "gunnysackers" end up only accelerating their anger by their stuffing-dumping cycle.

12. *Hitting below the belt*

This is the behavior we all fear the most for it is one of the most damaging of the angry behaviors. It can create a deep wound in a relationship, leaving a scar that is seldom forgotten. Usually it is used only as a last resort. When the pressure is on and the battle is hot, the spouse who feels he is losing ground will suddenly "hit below the belt." He will use his intimate knowledge of a sensitive issue to hit where it will hurt the most.

Sometimes this angry behavior is disguised in the form of a joke or a witty comment. If done in public, the momentary embarrassing silence that follows the "joke" indicates that not only did the spouse get the point, but so did those standing nearby. What adds to the effectiveness of this angry behavior is that the partner using it is giving a double message and can deny the maliciousness of the comment.

13. *Withholding*

This angry behavior is often used as a controlling form of punishment. Its mechanisms are quite simple—the person using this behavior merely withholds something important from his spouse. For example, a husband withholds money from his wife by keeping it in several checking accounts. The bank statements are sent to his office, so his wife has no idea what he makes or even what he spends. Whenever his wife needs money, for even such basic things as food or clothing for the kids, she almost has to beg in order to get him to respond. When the wife complains about his controlling behavior, he replies with something like, "I don't know why you're complaining, you have everything you need." Because his anger is so disguised, he cannot be objective enough to see the withholding pattern in his behavior and how it is affecting his relationship with his wife. Both husbands and wives can use this angry behavior by withholding other things, such as affection and sex. Regardless of what is withheld, this angry behavior only serves to increase the anger and resentment in the relationship.

In identifying these angry behaviors we can see that all of us have been guilty, at one time or another, of using them in our relationship with our spouse. We've also known what it is like to be on the receiving end, as well. The important thing to note, though, is that not one of them will help us build a stronger, closer, more intimate relationship. Yet when we get caught in the love-fear-anger cycle, we reach almost desperately for something with which to defend ourselves.

QUESTIONS TO CONSIDER:

1. List the three angry behaviors you use most often.
2. List the three angry behaviors you think your spouse uses most often.

3. Compare your lists with your spouse's list. Discuss signals you can use to alert each other when you sense that these angry behaviors may be surfacing in your relationship. How can you help each other avoid using these angry behaviors?

When I repress my emotions, my stomach keeps score.

JOHN POWELL

5

The Physical Side
of Anger

Looking over the list of angry behaviors in the last chapter, it appears that the most common way in which we attempt to handle our anger is simply to avoid it. Maybe we feel that if we can avoid it long enough, it will go away. This avoiding behavior is called repression, or suppression, and has an effect on us physically.

What does happen when we get angry? What goes on inside our body? A look at Webster's New World Dictionary gives us a starting point, and provides some interesting insight. The word *anger* is derived from the base *angh-,* which means "constricted, narrow, tightness, and distress." A few entries further down on the same page, the word *angina* is defined as any localized spasm of pain. It is derived from the base *angh-,* just as is anger, which links anger and angina. Even in ancient times, when language was still being developed, man saw that there was a connection between what he was experiencing physically and the emotion of anger.

The early research on anger focused primarily on this physical side of anger. One of the first studies of anger showed that a wide variety of physical symptoms accompanied the feeling of anger. People said that they felt either hot or cold, clenched their fists, and experienced sweating, choking, numbness, or twitching. Some people said they felt flush, while others said they felt pale. Some reported that their anger made them feel more alive and alert, while others said it made them feel afraid and even gave them headaches or nosebleeds.

Another early study observed the physical reactions in animals when they became afraid or angry. Both emotions caused physical changes. Digestion, assimilation, and elimination halted as the blood vessels to the stomach and intestines constricted, cutting off blood flow to these areas. Blood flow increased in the areas important in carrying out any decisions made as a result of anger: the brain, heart, lungs, and larger muscles in the arms and legs.

Researchers today have more sophisticated equipment available to help them in their study. Blood pressure, blood counts, brain waves, skin temperature, and heart rate are recorded in order to see what happens in the body when a person becomes angry. Some of these findings are summarized in an article in the June 1979 issue of *Changing Times:*

Consider the caveman. The sight of an enemy or dangerous animal sets off a series of hormonal and physical reactions. Adrenaline pours into his blood, speeding up his heartbeat and raising his blood pressure. Available fuel entering the blood as sugar increases, the red cells flood his bloodstream to transport more oxygen to the muscles and brain. Breathing accelerates to supply additional oxygen and to eliminate carbon dioxide created by sudden activity. Blood ordinarily required for digestion is shunted to the brain and muscles. Digestion slows. Pupils dilate, improving vision. Blood clotting ability accelerates, preparing for the possibility of a wound. All this gears the caveman for action to protect himself. In this aroused state he can stay and fight if the odds look good or flee if they don't.

Our bodies react the same way, though the danger is more likely to be a letter from the IRS than a saber-toothed tiger. And the threat doesn't have to be immediate to cause arousal. Merely anticipate anything unpleasant, perplexing or uncertain, and you can feel the stress reaction go off inside.

The article could have added that all or part of the physical reactions described for short-term emergencies can become an ongoing response to life as a result of repressed anger. Eventually, if we continue to bury our anger, the physical responses of long-term anger can create a breakdown within our bodies. Depending on our physical makeup, we may find ourselves suffering from any number of illnesses, ranging from mild elimination problems to hypertension or even cancer. It is only recently that we are finding out that anger can trigger other physical illnesses besides the occasional headache or an ulcer.

The extra adrenaline released into the blood stream was first identified by the researchers as the "anger hormone." As research continued, scientists found a second hormone released by the adrenal medulla, called noradrenaline. It seemed reasonable to suggest that each hormone was related to an emotional response, such as fear or anger.

A man named Albert Ax did some experiments in the early 1950s that seemed to support this idea. People volunteered for a project in his lab that involved elaborate measurements of heart rate, blood pressure, skin temperature, skin conductance, and muscle tension. After lying down on a table, the subjects were attached to the equipment for taking the measurements. They were told to just lie there and relax.

Suddenly, a problem developed with the equipment. Electrical sparks began to fly. The situation appeared to be very dangerous, perhaps even life threatening. All the lab personnel were busy trying to "fix" the equipment and no one paid any attention to the person wired up to the equipment. Finally, everything was restored to normal, and only then did one of the researchers check on the volunteer subject. Suddenly, another attendant entered the room with a very arrogant, irritating attitude. He was insulting to the researcher, the other attendants, and even to the volunteer who had just survived a very scary experience. But before anyone could react to his arrogance, he was gone.

The real purpose of the experiment was to produce a very frightening experience, followed by an incident designed to make the person angry. All the time, the equipment was taking measurements of the subject. When Ax analyzed the data collected, he found information that discriminated anger from fear. The symptoms of fear were very much like what would happen to a person if adrenaline was injected into his blood stream. The symptoms of anger were similar to what would be produced by an injection of both adrenaline and noradrenaline. For years, this study formed the basis for much of what we believed to be the physical side of anger. Later experiments, however, along with a closer look at the data in Ax's original study, showed that both hormones were involved in both emotions. Therefore, we cannot make a clear distinction between the physical effects of the emotion of fear and the emotion of anger. The only difference, physically, between the two is a matter of how intensely we react.

Both anger and fear are healthy emotions. They serve as warning systems that protect us from impending danger. But these two emotions, when left unresolved, can create physical damage to our body in the form of illness. When we look again at our love-anger-fear cycle, we see that two of the three are factors in the development of disease.

Building on the research of Dr. Meyer Friedman, which

identified Type A behavior as a cause of heart disease, and the work of Dr. Carl Simonton, in his research on cancer, doctors have come to realize that unresolved anger and fear play a role in both of these major killers. In fact, researchers are finding that, except in the case of a trauma, such as a car accident, or some other accidental injury, anger and fear play a role in almost all the physical damage done to our bodies. A specialist in psychosomatic illnesses, Harvard psychiatrist Dr. Silverman insists that a person cannot get sick without a stress factor's being involved. He identifies the buried emotions of anger and fear as the most important stress factors in physical illness.

What role do germs play in physical illnesses, then? Are they not the real cause of disease? What about the effects of air pollution and the carcinogenic particles that are supposed to cause cancer—where do they fit in? And what effect does diet have—isn't it an important factor? All of these are still important factors in illness, but they are not *the* critical factors. In studies done with identical twins who have the same genetic tendency toward an illness, or with people who breathe the same air or take into their bodies the same carcinogenic particles or eat the same diet—one might get sick while the other will not. The one who gets sick is generally the one exposed to an emotionally stressful situation in which overwhelming feelings of anger or fear are ignored.

Because of the personal emotional investment we make in our marriage, unresolved feelings of anger and fear in that relationship can make it one of the most stressful situations we can experience. Unless we find some way to effectively resolve these feelings, they can build to such an intensity that they can cause Type A behavior in any one of us. With Type A behavior, coronary heart disease can easily erupt in one's thirties or forties. Some people call Type A behavior the "hurry sickness" and feel that in order to avoid dealing with our feelings of anger or fear, we jump onto the treadmill of life. If we can go faster, we won't have to deal with anything. Because of this drive to get things done, or the continual time pressures we create, we simply add more things to be angry about—the cycle is complete. The faster we go, the more things we have to ignore. The more things we ignore, the more we experience anger or fear, and the faster we have to go in order to avoid these emotions. Medical researchers now identify this cycle as part of Type A behavior and see that any treatment plan must include the treatment of anger and fear if the healing process is to be complete.

What Dr. Friedman discovered about Type A behavior and heart disease, Dr. Carl Simonton has found to be equally true with cancer patients. The first trait that he and his team of researchers found to be at the root of cancer is a great tendency to hold in resentment and anger. In treating cancer patients, Dr. Simonton combines conventional medical treatment with psychotherapy. He and his associates insist on the psychotherapy in order to deal with buried anger. Often they see amazing remission of the disease as the person begins to deal effectively with that anger.

Another researcher, Dr. Robert Good, has shown that

cancer cells develop within each of us on a daily basis. But we do not develop the disease of cancer because the body's white blood cells stay busy as they continually attack and destroy these cancer cells before they can fully mature and take hold. The reason some people do develop cancer, according to Good, is the presence of emotional stressors, particularly unresolved anger. The hormones that the body releases under prolonged stress, including the hormone adrenaline, inhibit the body's normal ability to fight and destroy the cancer cells.

Simonton goes even further when he asserts that all illness, ranging from cancer to the common cold or a stomachache, is a result of the interaction of our body, our mind, and our emotions. According to him, the path to health and wellness begins when we take responsibility for our sickness. In order to do this, we must begin to work through the buried emotions of fear and anger. That's not a very comfortable concept. We may be able to help someone else work through his anger in order to prevent illness, but working through our own anger is another matter. That's probably why it stays hidden so long.

So it is clear that repressing anger—keeping it buried in the dark corners of our memory—is not a healthy way to handle that emotion. Yet we continue to avoid our anger, even though we can clearly see that that behavior is nonproductive. But what is our alternative? Does expressing our anger, or "letting it all hang out," provide any better results?

QUESTIONS TO CONSIDER:

1. Describe some of the physical symptoms you experience when you feel angry.
2. What physical "cues" do you see in your spouse that tell you that he/she is angry?
3. Think back to the last time you were sick. Could your illness have been related to your emotions? Why or why not?

*A person is praised who is angry
for the right reasons, with the right
people, and also in the right way, at
the right time, and for the right
length of time.*

ARISTOTLE

6

The Myths of Anger

Aristotle had the right idea—if only he had taken the time to tell us how to be angry the "right" way. Life would be a lot less complex if we could agree on the appropriate way to be angry. We've seen in the previous chapters that avoiding behaviors are ineffective ways to resolve anger and can cause physical illnesses as well. When we find that some particular pattern of behavior is destructive, our tendency is to look for alternative behaviors at the opposite end of the spectrum. If burying anger doesn't work, then let's lay it out on the table and see how that works.

Freud encouraged us in this direction. He said that we walk around with our conscious mind knowing less than half of what we are doing or why we are doing it. Our unconscious mind is really in control, and that deep, dark part of us is a churning cauldron of destructive impulses battling anything good within us. Those destructive impulses feed on our repressed emotions.

Freud saw aggression as a central part of our nature. At every stage of human development, we are supposed to be *enraged* at someone. Although he seldom said anything about anger directly, his ideas have filtered into our minds so that we link anger with aggression. His followers have come along and portrayed anger as the driving force behind most forms of aggression. They point out that anger is the emotion we feel when we have those aggressive impulses. These theorists imply that if a person does not become aggressive when angry, it is only because he is too inhibited to act out his aggressiveness.

Freud believed that when the emotion of anger comes to the surface of the unconscious and we become aware of it, we still do our best to push it back down below the surface. We do not want to face our repressed emotions. Some feel that perhaps we do this because we have been taught by example to avoid our anger, or we have learned through painful and embarrassing experiences how dangerous our anger can become. Keeping anger in the unconscious may work for a short period of time, but eventually anger seems to fester and explode when we least expect it. This has led theorists to encourage us to become aware of our anger and get it out on the table before it can explode.

Although Freud was speaking about aggression metaphorically, many of his ideas have been taken literally. One of the most familiar concepts is the "hydraulic" theory of anger. This theory assumes that stored emotions become like a hydraulic system, something like the brakes on a car. When you push on one area, something has to give in another area. Stored-up anger will come bursting out in some unpredictable manner when someone pushes us the wrong way.

Closely related to the "hydraulic" theory is the "reservoir" theory. This approach maintains that when we repress an emotion like anger, it is stored up in some huge reservoir. Unless we find some way to let out our anger, it will grow to enormous proportions, seeping or bursting out of the reservoir of the unconscious at the most inappropriate time, ruining some important relationship.

Although these ideas sound logical, and may even "feel right," they have never been supported by the results of research. In spite of this, many counselors ignore this lack of empirical support and tell their clients that it is dangerous to "dam up" any feelings, as this may cause them to "spill over," either in the form of neurotic or other inappropriate behavior.

Some of the leaders in popular psychology have taken these ideas a step further and have encouraged us to *ventilate* our emotions, particularly the emotion of anger. The hydraulic theory and the reservoir theory are rather passive ways of handling our emotions—the feelings "just overflow" all by themselves. But ventilating our emotions is a more active method, which advises, "Don't just let it seep out, actively do something to release the tension!" Expressions like "let it all hang out" are an encouragement to "let the anger out." If we could only actively *ventilate* our anger in some way, we might be able to get rid of that anger—we might experience catharsis. It seems like a reasonable set of ideas—if damming up our anger causes it to fester and grow, then actively ventilating our anger should cause it to diminish.

A whole range of behaviors has been identified as being cathartic: vigorous physical activity, such as running, exercise, or sports; throwing dishes; beating pillows; fantasizing revenge; or even kicking a stone. It is believed that if you can experience the release of physical energy through these behaviors, you can also experience release from pent-up anger. Even the National Association for Mental Health advocates this type of behavior. One of their suggestions for resolving stressful emotions is "Work off your anger. Cool it for a day or two while expending physical energy in a do-it-yourself project around the house, playing tennis, or taking long walks." Unfortunately, when we try to experience the release of anger through physical release, we usually end up still being angry.

Some of the advocates of ventilating anger add another dimension in their approach. They have changed the cry of "Express yourself," to "Look out for number one!" If you are looking out for yourself, ventilating anger can feel pretty good. "I feel so much better" is the testimony of those who have just expressed their anger. But check back later and you will find the anger still hanging around. Of course, some people are not too concerned with several days from now, or that the problem still remains unresolved—just so they feel better.

The idea of expressing anger, or ventilating it, is not new to this generation. Its roots go way back in time. Aristotle wrote on anger in order to help orators control the anger sometimes aroused in the audience by a speech and expressed in shouting back at the speaker. William Blake, an eighteenth century English poet and artist, wrote a poem that expressed some of the ideas of the ventilationists. He wrote:

> I was angry with my friend;
> I told my wrath, my wrath did end.
> I was angry with my foe:
> I hid my wrath, my wrath did grow.

Blake was a good poet and even a good philosopher for the "ventilationist school" of thinking, but he overlooked some of the same things the advocates of ventilating anger also overlook. Sometimes there are situations in which we want to hide our wrath from a friend because the value of that friendship far outweighs the importance of what made us angry. Does that mean our wrath will not end? Or what about the situation where in our rage, we express our wrath to a foe, who also happens to outweigh us by a hundred pounds? Expressing anger in that situation just might increase the other person's anger to the point of endangering our physical well-being. The poem, along with the advice of the ventilationists, doesn't always fit in with our experiences.

In spite of these inconsistencies, the ventilationists

would lead us to believe that not only do we clear our arteries when we express our anger, we help to improve the quality of our relationships as well. Marriage counselors are quick to jump on the bandwagon and tell marriage partners that it is healthy for them to express their anger to each other. But in marriage after marriage, the outcome is the same—the angry outburst is followed by louder and louder accusations, then crying or screaming, until one or both people give up through sheer exhaustion. Then one may offer a reluctant apology, or both may just settle into a moody silence that is a welcomed relief from the shouting. But the silence is only a quiet recess, for the next day, or several days or weeks later, the scene is repeated. Nothing is changed. Nobody really feels any better, and neither the problem nor the anger has gone away.

Most of the advocates of the ventilation theory would never advocate screaming matches. That is what is called "dirty fighting." Instead, they seek to control the expression of anger, seeing it as a helpful form of communication. Expressing our anger means we say to our spouse something like, "Get out of my way—I'm looking for a fight." Whether this is stated verbally, or is expressed through nonverbal behavior, it hardly sounds like a very constructive form of communication.

The point overlooked by the ventilationists is that merely expressing anger does nothing to effectively resolve it. Study after study shows that only when the expression or ventilation of anger leads directly to a resolution of the problem causing that anger, does this type of behavior lead to a reduction of anger.

Some of the "milder" advocates among the ventilationists attempt to pull us closer to what they see as the center of the spectrum. They say the solution is to "talk over your anger." That sounds like a reasonable form of expressing anger. Talking things over with a sympathetic listener, such as a good friend, should make one feel better. But once again, these theorists end up in another blind alley, for they overlook the fact that efforts to "talk through" anger are really efforts to justify our point of view. That's why talking out anger with a friend, or even with a therapist, seldom reduces anger. Instead, it causes us to rehearse in our mind the situation that originally triggered the anger. This in turn can give us a clearer picture of why we feel justified in our anger. And we end up just as angry, or perhaps even more so than before, because we have received support in justification of our anger.

The next time you try to talk out your anger with a friend, notice what you are feeling as you talk with your sympathetic listener. Notice what happens each time she agrees with you. As you talk through your anger, you will probably become aware of more of the nuances surrounding the anger-triggering event. Your sympathetic listener nods her head in agreement, not only in agreement with what you are feeling, but also with your right to feel that anger. Your anger becomes more defined, and in turn, you may even begin to feel more angry than you did when you started to "talk through" your anger.

The same thing can happen when you attempt to talk through your anger with your spouse. In this situation, instead of receiving sympathy from your listener, you will probably receive a defensive statement—one in which your partner defends his right to act the way he did, or say what he said. The more he defends his right to behave as he did, the more you have to defend your right to be angry. The result is more and more anger.

It appears that it is becoming harder and harder to identify good reasons to be angry, or to find the right time to be angry, let alone the right *way* to be angry. Aristotle's advice offers little help in sorting through the myths surrounding anger. It is clear that expressing anger, even by talking it through, is not the solution. Venting anger can actually increase the anger being experienced. And talking through anger may only serve to paralyze us in our angry state of mind. These behaviors that propose to offer a solution to anger seem to be no improvement over the possibility that physical illness can result from holding anger in.

QUESTIONS TO CONSIDER:

1. What are some of the theories you have heard about that relate to expressing anger?
2. What are your thoughts and feelings about "marital fighting"? Discuss them with your spouse.
3. Can you remember times when you have tried to "talk through" your anger and failed? What contributed to your inability to resolve the anger in that situation?

Do you do well to be angry?

JONAH 4:4

7

Understanding Anger Through Self-Talk

Most of us look at our feelings and relate how we feel to the events in our lives. If good things happen to us, we feel happy and satisfied. If bad things happen to us, we feel angry or hurt. As a result, we spend considerable effort trying to rearrange the circumstances of our lives in order to insure a happy marriage situation.

But a moment's reflection on the most recent happening that made us feel angry with our spouse will help us see the problem with such reasoning. Think of what your spouse did that made you angry. Can you think of a time when he or she did that very same thing and you did not get angry? Perhaps you were feeling so good about everything else that you simply ignored that offending behavior. Or maybe you can even think of a time when you chuckled to yourself about the same behavior that recently infuriated you.

The truth is that our emotions and behavior are *not* dependent on what is going on around us. Our spouse can change, or the circumstances can change but we will still get angry. We can even change spouses, only to find that the problem with anger increases. The reason is that there is something else at work that determines why we get angry. This additional factor exists right inside us—between the ears. It is our thoughts, or what I call Self-Talk.*

The *ABC*'s of Anger

Most of us blame our emotions on our circumstances. "If you knew my spouse, you'd know why I'm angry!" "She makes me *so* mad!" "I'm fed up with his stupid behavior— I've had it!" If we haven't said or thought these exact statements, we have probably come pretty close. We almost instinctively believe that external circumstances cause us to feel what we feel.

In looking at the *ABC*'s of anger, Albert Ellis calls these external circumstances the *Activating* events or experiences, or the *A* in our *ABC*'s. The anger we generally associate with these *Activating* events or experiences are the emotional *Consequences*, or the *C* in our *ABC*'s. We interpret life as if it were like this:

* The ideas in the following section are explained in greater detail in our book *Self-Talk: Key to Personal Growth.*

A causes C

For example, your husband didn't take the time to call you from the office today, and you feel hurt and angry. That's like saying:

A (His failure to phone you) causes C (I feel hurt and angry)

Other examples could include:

A (The house is a mess)   causes C (I am angry because she doesn't seem to care)

A (He yelled at the kids)   causes C (I'm frustrated and feel helpless)

A (She bounced a check)   causes C (She makes me so angry! Why can't she be more careful, especially when I work so hard?)

There are countless other examples you could write into the parentheses:

A (   ) causes C (   )
A (   ) causes C (   )
A (   ) causes C (   )

However, when we accept the idea that *A causes C*, we are ignoring our *ABC*'s! If we know our alphabet, we can see that there is a *B* that comes between the *A* and the *C;* and the *B* is the key. *B* refers to our <u>*belief systems*</u>—our thought patterns—which is our Self-Talk. It is these thoughts (which come and go so quickly that we hardly notice them) that are the cause of our anger and angry responses to our spouse. Look again at our first example:

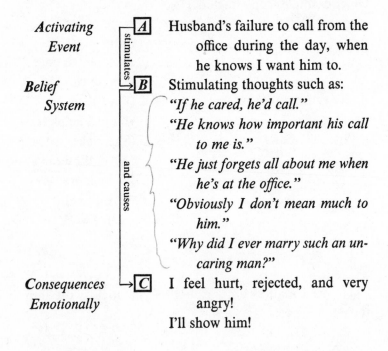

Activating Event	A *stimulates*	Husband's failure to call from the office during the day, when he knows I want him to.
Belief System	→B	Stimulating thoughts such as: *"If he cared, he'd call."* *"He knows how important his call to me is."* *"He just forgets all about me when he's at the office."* *"Obviously I don't mean much to him."* *"Why did I ever marry such an uncaring man?"*
Consequences Emotionally	→C	I feel hurt, rejected, and very angry! I'll show him!

A more accurate formula for understanding our anger is

<u>*A* stimulates *B* which causes *C*</u>

Of course activating experiences trigger the process. For example, if you are expected to work full-time *and* cook *and* keep the house clean and are told so, this circumstance or activating event will contribute significantly to the emotional consequence. You probably would not be feeling anger if you had not perceived the occurrence of the activating event. But your husband's expectations cannot *directly* cause you to be angry, because in your thoughts—your Self-Talk—you have some degree of choice. You could choose to react in your Self-Talk with various non-angry observations, such as (1) "My husband is unreasonable. Too bad!"; (2) "I don't like his attitude, but I can handle it"; and (3) "I am sad that my husband doesn't understand my needs. But I think I can help him deal with me more fairly in the future."

Using one of these thoughts, or "belief systems," you will still have an emotional response to your husband as he sits reading the paper while you do the dishes, but it won't be anger. You may feel disappointed, annoyed, or even strongly displeased at his behavior, but not hostile, resentful, or filled with rage. In order to feel angry at your husband, you would have to think different thoughts. The anger-producing thoughts, in the above example, would include (1) "What an *awful* way to treat me!" (2) "He's so unfair! Anyone who treats a mate as he does is acting *horribly!*" (3) "He *should* know I work hard too!" and (4) "I can't stand his behavior! He'd better shape up *or else!*"

Notice that each of these statements, and just about every other anger-producing thought we can say to ourselves about our spouse, or anyone, contains an absolutistic element. Even when it is not stated directly, there is always a demand in the belief systems that leads to anger. Notice the first statement: What is implied is that "He shouldn't treat me that way!" Implied in the second statement is the thought "My husband shouldn't treat me unfairly!" And in the fourth statement, what is implied is "If he cares about me, he should act like it!"

The key to understanding anger is to understand that "obscene" word *should*. Every time we feel frustration or hurt that leads to anger, we can connect our anger to the "shoulds" in our Self-Talk. These "shoulds" are a demand on our spouse. Of course, these "shoulds" can be expressed in a negative way as "shouldn'ts" with the same effect.

There are other words that are derivatives of the "shoulds," and these are words and phrases like *must, got to, ought to,* and so forth. They all do the same thing—they trigger anger. And they do this because when we use them, we are making a demand on a situation or a person that we cannot effectively guarantee will be met. When we set up these demands within our Self-Talk, we create an emotional tension within that creates anger.

Are you angry with your spouse? Look for the "shoulds" or "shouldn'ts." The first step in defusing your anger is to identify those demands and change them into wants and desires.

Let's go back to the wife in our example again. The same situation with her husband occurs several days later. Only this time the wife is aware of the effect of her "shoulds." So instead of making those demands on her husband in her Self-Talk, she creates Self-Talk in the form of wants and desires. Now she thinks and says things like

> "I wish my husband was more understanding about how tired I am."
> "It would make our marriage so much better if he could understand my feelings."
> "Life would sure be more pleasant in the evenings around here if he would pitch in and help."

You might read over this list and the first list of thoughts to see if they each create a different type of feeling inside you. The last list still does not guarantee that the wife will get what she wants. That's not the purpose in changing our Self-Talk. What it does do is reduce the inner-tension level, and that frees some emotional energy to find creative ways to deal with the situation. She may still have some feelings of frustration, or sadness, or hurt. But those feelings do not paralyze her the way anger can if she does not resolve it in her thoughts.

But "shouldn't" her husband be more helpful and understanding? Probably. But placing those demands on him in her thoughts is an irrational process for the wife. Why? There are at least three reasons why.

First, whenever we are angry about something with our spouse, our "shoulds," or demands, are usually directed to the *past*. Notice what she thought: "He shouldn't act that way!" Can her demands on him change the fact that he has *already* acted that way? Of course not. What is past, is. It can't be changed. But examine your Self-Talk. Aren't most of your "shoulds" and "musts" related to the past? It is irrational to make demands on the past, for the past cannot be changed.

But what about the future? He shouldn't act that way in the future! But notice what happens when the wife verbalizes her demand to her husband. She says something like this:

> "You are unfair! I work too, and you should help me in the evenings!"

Her husband will probably reply:

> "Hey, I'm beat. My work is physical! I don't just sit behind a desk all day!"

Or, he might come up with any number of replies, all designed to defend his right to sit and read the newspaper, or watch TV. And what is the wife going to do? Get angry! Why? Because the **second** reason the demands are irrational is that we *cannot enforce* the demands we make on our spouse. We end up being confronted with our own helplessness.

But what if the wife is *really* angry and makes some threats? Then she will probably encounter the **third** reason why the demands are irrational: If we try to enforce our demands on our spouse, we will encounter *resistance*. Oh, tomorrow he might try to help a little, but then he'll probably get home a little later, or find something that needs to be done out in the garage, or maybe he'll have a terrible headache. There are countless other passive ways he can resist the demands made by his wife.

It seems to be human nature to resist the "shoulds" in life. We not only resist the ones placed there by our spouse, we even resist the "shoulds" we place on ourselves. All "shoulds" are irrational! Only God can place a demand on us, for He's the only one I know who has the power to enforce the demand. People just don't have that kind of power.

But, you might be saying, that's no way to live. There should be some "shoulds!" There must be! Not if you want to resolve your anger. The absence of "shoulds" seems to fit very nicely into what Jesus says in Matthew 5:38–45:

> You have heard that it was said, "An eye for an eye and a tooth for a tooth." But I say to you, Do not resist one who is evil. But if any one strikes you on the right cheek, turn to him the other also; and if any one would sue you and take your coat, let him have your cloak as well; and if any one forces you to go one mile, go with him two miles. Give to him who begs from you, and do not refuse him who would borrow from you.
>
> You have heard that it was said, "You shall love your neighbor and hate your enemy." But I say to you, Love your enemies and pray for those who persecute you, so that you may be sons of your Father who is in heaven; for he makes his sun rise on

the evil and on the good, and sends rain on the just
and on the unjust.

Don't resist, Jesus says, Don't sit there and grovel in
your anger; get up and go beyond the law. Love your
enemy, for the only thing that matters is to be a child of the
Father. We are not to worry about what is fair in life; no
one ever said life would be fair. And in spite of our dreams
and expectations, no one can guarantee that marriage will
be fair, either. Yet we continue to make demands and end
up angry. That anger only serves to paralyze us into inac-
tivity; or it spills out in harsh words that lead to further
hurt and anger.

If your spouse does something, and you make a demand
in your Self-Talk that he *shouldn't* do it, you'll get angry.
Jesus says, go the extra mile. Obviously, I don't believe He
wants you to stand there and take something that is harm-
ful or dangerous. That is foolishness. What I believe He
is talking about is an attitude of compromise and empathy.
It is a pattern of thinking that does away with the demands, allowing them to exist only in the form of wants
and desires. So instead of saying things in her mind like

"He is so unfair!"
"He'd better get his act together quickly!"
"I shouldn't have to put up with that!"

the wife changes her Self-Talk into thoughts like these:

"I sure wish he could see how I'm feeling."
"It would be so nice if he would help me."

"I want him to be willing to share this work with me. Maybe I can talk to him when we're both not so tired."

Those kinds of thoughts may not sound very natural, but they are the kind of Self-Talk that will dissolve her anger. And when her anger is lessened, she can speak those thoughts to him; and he just might hear her for a change.

She may still have some feelings of frustration, or sadness, or hurt. But those feelings will not paralyze her the way her anger will if left unresolved. When you feel frustrated, sad, or hurt, you are still able to temper those feelings with compassion. And without the anger, you will be able to find some creative ways to communicate your wishes and desires to your spouse in a way that will maximize the possibility of his really hearing you.

Here is a helpful way to organize your Self-Talk, to analyze your "shoulds," and then to change the "shoulds" into wishes, wants, and desires. Take an 8½ x 11 sheet of paper, turn it sideways and make three columns. In the first column, make a list of all the things that your spouse does that trigger feelings of anger within you. Don't write them out in detail, just make a brief note of what it is so you can identify it when you look at the paper later.

In the second column, identify the demands you are making on your spouse in that situation. What are the "shoulds" you have in your mind—what is it your spouse really "should" or "shouldn't" be doing. Then, in the third column, rewrite the demand statements in the form of wishes, wants, or desires. See the examples on page 108.

Things I am angry about in relation to my spouse	Identify the demands I am making on my spouse	Restate the demands as wishes, wants, or desires
When I fix a "romantic" meal, he hardly notices. He can't wait for it to end and get to his newspaper.	He *should* want to spend time with me. He *should* recognize that I need attention from him. He *should* appreciate my hard work.	I wish he would notice when I have candles on the table, and be willing to sit and talk with me for a bit. I really wish he would make a fire in the fireplace as I clear the table, and that we could sit by the fire together for even thirty minutes.
He's so rude around my family.	He *should* be polite. After all, I'm nice to his parents. He *should* do the same for me.	It would be so nice if he could be nice to my parents. I wish he could be a little more patient with them.
She's always on my back to do odd jobs around the house. I'll do them when I'm ready!	She *should* get off my back! She should know how tired I am from work. She *should* just know that I'll eventually get around to it!	I sure wish she'd let me decide what I need to do around the house. It would be so nice if she would just trust me when I say I will do it.

In your Self-Talk, you need to argue against the demands. Remind yourself of the three reasons the demands are irrational.

Make the list as long as you can. I had one couple work on making individual angry lists, and the man ended up with over fifty pages—all about his wife! He had a lot of repressed anger. You don't have to write as many pages as he did, but see if you can do at least several pages.

There are two important things you can do with your anger list. The first thing is to get the list out every time you begin to feel angry about a particular situation and read over the three columns, paying particular attention to the third column. This process of reading and rereading the list will help you understand the steps you take in your Self-Talk to identify the demands, recognize they are irrational, and restate the demands as wishes, wants, and desires. After some practice, you will be able to do the same processing and restating within your mind, capturing every thought and "should" and bringing it into obedience to Christ.

The second thing you can do with the list is to sit down with your spouse at an agreed-upon time and begin to work slowly through some of the important items on each other's list. When you do this, do not go into great detail about the items listed in the first column. The only purpose in referring to the first column is to make certain your spouse knows what situation you are talking about. Then, and this is most important, *skip over the second column!* Go immediately to the third column and share the thoughts you have listed in that column. An amazing thing often happens. When you begin to talk to your spouse in the language of wishes, wants and desires—without the demands of the "shoulds"—the other person actually begins to hear what you are saying. Your spouse understands what is important to you.

Sometimes, you can state what is in the third column, but still have the demands implied in what you say or feel. It is like saying, "I really wish you would . . . (and you better do it, because you should!)" Getting rid of the "shoulds" means you *really let go* of your demands and expectations. It may take several sessions talking together before the "shoulds" are not only eliminated from the conversation, but are also not implied. At that point, you will begin to communicate effectively with each other about the areas that have previously triggered angry responses in your relationship. For some of you, though, there are areas that will take more than an angry list to resolve, for sometimes anger can lead to resentment and bitterness.

QUESTIONS TO CONSIDER:

1. What are some of the areas in your relationship in which you are having difficulty identifying the "shoulds"? Talk about these areas with your spouse.
2. What are some of the "shoulds" you receive from your spouse? How could you be helped by changing them into wishes, wants, or desires?
3. Decide what will be the first "should" you are going to eliminate in your relationship with your spouse. Share it with him/her.

Only the heart knows its own bitterness, and no stranger shares its joy.

PROVERBS 14:10

8

The Way of Forgiveness

Anger is an insistence on my right to make demands on life, or God, or other people, or on my spouse. If we persist in making those demands, our anger can become resentment. Over time, this unresolved anger can put its roots down deep within us, leading to cynicism and bitterness.

There is a story in the Bible, found in Joshua 7, which illustrates the results of buried feelings of resentment and bitterness. Prior to the events in Joshua 7, the Israelites had captured and destroyed the city of Jericho. God had given them very specific instructions about the spoils of that battle. Only the silver and gold, and the vessels of bronze and iron, were to be taken—everything else was to be destroyed. The captured "loot" would be placed in the treasury of the Lord.

Now back in those days, soldiers were paid with the

"loot" they could capture. But the army of Israel was told that at Jericho, there would be no "loot." Unbeknown to Joshua, one of the Israelite soldiers had disobeyed those instructions, which led to some very serious results.

Following the victory at Jericho, Joshua sent some men up to the next city, called Ai. They came back and told Joshua that Ai would be a pushover. "Let not all the people go up, but let about two or three thousand men go up and attack Ai . . . for they are but few" (verse 3), was their advice. And so it was. Joshua sent three thousand men to do battle against Ai. But instead of an easy victory, the men of Israel fled from the men of Ai, and thirty-six Israelites were killed. When the people heard this, ". . . the hearts of the people melted, and became as water" (verse 5). Fear took control.

In desperation, Joshua took his case to the Lord. "Alas, O Lord God," he prayed, "why hast thou brought this people over the Jordan at all, to give us into the hands of the Amorites, to destroy us? Would that we had been content to dwell beyond the Jordan!" (verse 7). Now Joshua was a great man of faith, but his complaint sounds very much like the complaints of the people as they wandered through the wilderness. "Would to God we had stayed in Egypt" could have been their theme song.

One of the times the people complained, they wanted water. By the time Moses responded to their complaints, he was angry with them. God told Moses to speak to the rock and it would give water for the people, but Moses was angry. Instead of speaking to the rock, he struck it several times with his rod. Water came forth abundantly for the people, but God had to punish Moses for his disobedience and anger. The place where this happened was named Meribah, or bitterness. (*See* Numbers 20.)

Joshua spent the whole day upon his face before the ark of the Lord. All the elders of Israel were with him. Finally God responded to his prayer, but not quite the way Joshua expected. It almost seemed as though God was patiently waiting for Joshua to finish with his demands; and finally God said to him, "Get up, Joshua, stop wasting your time and mine with praying. There is a problem in the camp of Israel that needs fixing. This is not the time to pray!" (*see* verses 10–15).

Joshua got caught in the trap that so many of us get caught in. When trouble strikes, we want to *try harder*. And as we have already pointed out, trying harder only gets you more of the same. Joshua tried harder, with praying, by putting dust and ashes upon his head, by complaints and pleas to God, but all he got was more and more frustration. Why? Because the problem was not between God and Joshua, the problem was in the camp of Israel. Something had gone wrong. And until that problem was faced, nothing would change.

What was the problem in Israel? God told Joshua He would point out the person responsible for the problem. That person was a man named Achan. Poor Achan—how he must have felt during the process of elimination that left him standing alone! He knew he had been the cause of the problem, and he knew the penalty for what he had done.

As Joshua stood before that lonely man Achan, notice what he told him, "My son, give glory to the Lord God of Israel, and render praise to him; and tell me now what you have done . . ." (verse 19). Confess, Joshua told him. Notice the context of his request. He told Achan his confession would give glory and praise to God. So Achan confessed that he stole from the "loot" of Jericho, and that the shekels of silver, the bar of gold, and the robe were *buried* in the earth inside his tent.

The rest of the chapter in Joshua tells us that Achan, his family, and all that he possessed were taken to the Valley of Achor, where they were stoned to death and then burned. What a horrible price to pay for some "treasure" that lay buried in the earth inside his tent. Such a small thing, but then it is always the little things that ensnare us and do us in.

The point in reviewing this story is not to comment on the problems of coveting a little silver, some gold, or a beautiful Babylonian robe. Let's look instead at the effect of the little things that lie buried deep within the earth inside the tent of our life. When we dig down, we discover hidden resentments, forgotten hurts, and buried feelings of bitterness that have been carefully nursed over the years.

Perhaps it is these "little" things that are the remaining barriers to intimacy in our marriage, even though we have carefully worked through our anger lists. What often happens when we scrape away the anger is that we come face-to-face with buried feelings of resentment and bitterness.

Bitterness is a poison that eventually destroys us, affects

our mates, and even people who are not involved in our
life. The buried "treasure" of Achan left thirty-six men
dead, and then led to the death of his family and himself.
That's why the writer to the Hebrews warns us to be careful, for "there can very easily spring up ... a bitter spirit
which is not only bad in itself, but can also poison the lives
of others" (Hebrews 12:15 PHILLIPS).

How does anger grow into bitterness? It begins with a
hurt, or a *frustration:* A harsh word spoken to me when I
feel vulnerable; being frustrated because my partner fails
to say the right thing, or fails to do something very mean-
ingful for me; something said in the heat of an argument
that I cannot forget—all of these are part of the hurts we
experience in a relationship. Some of these hurts and frustrations have been erased over the years simply because we
overlook them, or forget them, but others stay behind and
take root in the private places inside our tent.

The second step in the way of bitterness is the *complaining* stage. Here we often are willing to express our feelings
of hurt and disappointment. This is also the stage in which
we may first become aware of being angry. Job experienced this stage when he said, "I will not restrain my
mouth; I will speak in the anguish of my spirit; I will com-
plain in the bitterness of my soul" (Job 7:11). We have already seen that talking about our anger can make us more
angry. Job says he will not restrain his mouth—he will talk
and talk about his hurt and anger, feeding the roots of bitterness within his tent.

The third step in the way of bitterness is to pull it all

back within us. This stage is called the *nursing* stage, or the stage of *quiet* resentment. Nothing is said, except within the privacy of our own mind. The proverb quoted at the beginning of the chapter tells us that "The heart knows its own bitterness, and no stranger shares its joy" (Proverbs 14:10). What an interesting combination of thoughts—the joy of bitterness. It is almost as if there is a morbid enjoyment in nursing anger and complaints, massaging them into the ground of our tent and feeding the root of our bitterness. No one knows it is there except us, but what we are left with is a bitter spirit that builds a wall that shuts out intimacy.

The behaviors of anger that we discussed in the fourth chapter fit into this process. All of those behaviors cause hurts and frustrations. If nothing is done to break the cycle of those behaviors, we create within us or within our spouse a cynical attitude toward marriage and intimacy and then eventually a bitterness that isolates us from the person we love. And the source of it all is anger.

The *way of bitterness* might be pictured as on the following page.

A bitter spirit can end up building a wall that isolates us from the people we love and from those who love us. An example of a bitter spirit, and the lonely results of that bitterness, is seen in the character of Saul, Israel's first king. Soon after we meet Saul in 1 Samuel 9, we find him faced with a seemingly unresolvable stalemate. The Philistines had a giant of a man, named Goliath, who had the Israelite

THE WAY OF BITTERNESS

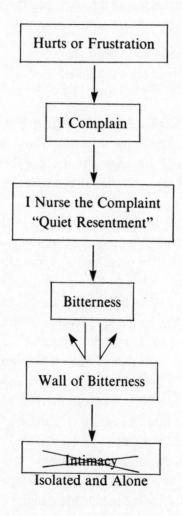

army paralyzed. The story of how young David killed Goliath is well-known. The events following that victory are
not.

David's fame as a warrior grew, and the women sang in
the streets a song that went as follows:

> Saul has slain his thousands,
> and David his ten thousands.
>
> 1 SAMUEL 18:7

When Saul heard the people singing this song, he "was
very angry." The song displeased him, and instead of
working through his anger, Saul chose the way of bitterness. Verse 9 says that "Saul eyed David from that day
on."

Angry complaints that were nursed in the quietness of
the mind became bitterness. The wall that was erected not
only blocked out the person who supposedly triggered that
anger, it broadened and affected other important relationships as well. David became a close friend to Jonathan,
Saul's son. Then he married Michal, Saul's daughter. But
all this time, Saul nursed his anger at David. Soon that
anger and bitterness turned against his own son Jonathan.
In 1 Samuel 20:30 we read that "Saul's anger was kindled
against Jonathan." The wall of bitterness closed in around
Saul, isolating him from his own children.

When David was forced to flee for his life, Saul's anger
against David threatened to consume him. All he could
think of was how to kill David. After disgracing his son
Jonathan, Saul took Michal, his daughter, David's wife,

and gave her to another man. (*See* 1 Samuel 25:44.) All of his behavior was controlled by his irrational passion. On two occasions, David had the opportunity to kill Saul, but out of loyalty and reverence for Saul's position as king, David allowed him to live. When David let Saul know that he could have killed him, Saul's goal remained the same—David had to be destroyed. One can almost imagine Saul sitting in the corner of his tent late at night, nursing his anger and bitterness, and then burying it in the ground. Lonely and bitter, Saul ended up destroying himself as the wall of bitterness that he built over the years collapsed in upon him.

So what is the solution to the way of bitterness? How can we avoid the loneliness and isolation that we experience behind the wall of bitterness? The solution to bitterness, and to the anger which forms the foundation of bitterness, is *forgiveness.*

"But I've tried to forgive," you say, "and only end up back in the tent quietly nursing the hurt and bitterness. How can I really learn to forgive?" Just as there is a way of bitterness, there is also a *way of forgiveness.*

The way of forgiveness begins with putting an end to the blame game. The blame game seeks to finger the culprit. I try to show that you are to blame, and you try to show that I am to blame. We are both trying to assign the role of villain to the other person, perhaps so that we can extract some kind of punishment. But placing blame never helps. As we have pointed out, in any disagreement, *both people are right!* Neither one may be *correct,* in that they accurately perceived what took place, but both are *right* in their perceptions.

In the blame game, no one wins; but we find it very difficult to let go of our demands. Our demands are so obviously just, just because they are ours. And the demands that are the hardest to let go of are the ones that insist that you see things as I see them, that you think as I think, or that you feel as I feel. If we hang on to these demands, we will hang on to the blame game. We cannot even consider forgiveness when we are still blaming.

The next step in the way of forgiveness is to make forgiveness a way of life. How do we do that? Perhaps that is the question Peter had in mind when in Matthew 18:21, he asked Jesus, "Lord, how often shall my brother sin against me, and I forgive him? As many as seven times?" It's as if he was saying, "Lord, how many times do I have to go through this process of forgiving my spouse? Isn't there a point where I can stop?" And Jesus said to him, "No, not seven times, but seventy times seven" (*see* Matthew 18:22). Four hundred and ninety times? Yes, Peter, four hundred and ninety times! And one old manuscript adds the idea that we are to forgive four hundred and ninety times each day!

What Jesus is saying is that it is not a question of how many times we are to forgive, but that forgiveness is to become a way of life—the way of forgiveness. If you want to get rid of the roots of bitterness, and dig up that corner of the tent and plant something nice there, you make forgiveness a part of the way you live.

Following His answer to Peter, Jesus then relates a parable that illustrates the point He has just made. Beginning at verse 23, He says:

> The Kingdom of Heaven can be compared to a king who decided to bring his accounts up to date. In the process, one of his debtors was brought in who owed him $10,000,000! He couldn't pay, so the king ordered him sold for the debt, also his wife and children and everything he had.
>
> But the man fell down before the king, his face in the dust, and said, "Oh, sir, be patient with me and I will pay it all."
>
> Verses 23–26 TLB

What an insurmountable task! He owes his master $10 million, and all he can do is ask for a little more time. Perhaps he is thinking, "I'll try a little harder! I should have written him a letter explaining the situation."

> Then the king was filled with pity for him and released him and *forgave his debt.*
>
> Verse 27 TLB

Incredible! Forgiven of $10 million! That is real forgiveness. If that had been me, I'd have been a new man, but look at him:

> But when the man left the king, he went to a man who owed him $2,000 and grabbed him by the

> throat and demanded instant payment. The man
> fell down before him and begged him to give him a
> little time. "Be patient and I will pay it," he pled.
>
> Verses 28,29 TLB

Now you would think a little red light would go on in
that man's head reminding him that he had just said the
same thing to the king. The king had forgiven an incredible debt—a life-changing experience. But not so in this
case.

> But his creditor wouldn't wait. He had the man
> arrested and jailed until the debt would be paid in
> full.
>
> Then the man's friends went to the king and told
> him what had happened. And the king called be-
> fore him the man he had forgiven and said, "You
> evil-hearted wretch! Here I forgave you all that
> tremendous debt, just because you asked me to—
> shouldn't you have mercy on others, just as I had
> mercy on you?"
>
> Then the angry king sent the man to the torture
> chamber until he had paid every last penny due. So
> shall my heavenly Father do to you if you refuse to
> truly forgive your brothers.
>
> Verses 30–34 TLB

I think what the king was saying to this man was,
"Didn't you understand that I forgave you? Didn't you feel

the extent of that forgiveness? Apparently not, for the man acted as one who still owed a huge debt. He never made forgiveness a part of his life-style.

Jesus is saying in this parable that the real issue is not how often we are to forgive, but how can we dare *not* forgive. In God's eyes, each one of us is a multiple offender—we owe a tremendous debt! But God in His grace has forgiven the debt we owe—a debt which we could never repay regardless of how much time we have. If we have been forgiven like that, how can we withhold forgiveness from anyone?

If the way of bitterness is an insistence on the right to make demands, then the way of forgiveness is a letting go of those rights. The man in the parable never understood that. He said, "God may forgive me a debt that I could never repay, but I *can't* forgive *that person* in *that situation!* I will never forgive!" How sad! That is the way of bitterness, not the way of forgiveness.

The *way of forgiveness* might be pictured as on the following page.

The life-style of forgiveness is a way of living that eliminates any possibility of a root of bitterness taking hold within us. We can only walk in the way of forgiveness by experiencing God's forgiveness, and then forgiving our spouse, and others, as God has forgiven us.

Our understanding of forgiveness must parallel our insight into our experience of being forgiven by God. We enter into God's forgiveness by recognizing that we stand in the presence of one who loves us unconditionally. As we

THE WAY OF FORGIVENESS

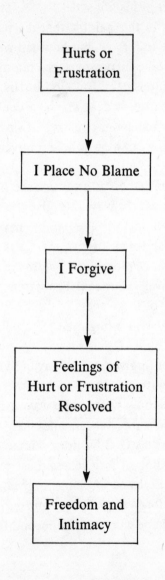

realize that God's love toward us is unconditional, we are free to respond to Him and accept His forgiveness. As we experience forgiveness, reconciliation occurs. We who were enemies are now at peace with each other (*see* Romans 5:6–11).

An exciting thing happens when we experience being loved unconditionally. We can see ourselves as valued persons, who are prized and cared for by the other. Love forms the foundation for forgiveness and is also the fruit of forgiveness as well.

The same thing can occur in our marriage. As we begin to let go of the demands we make on our partner, our love becomes more unconditional. Then we are each free to respond to love that is freely offered by our partner, so we begin to turn toward that love. We forgive, and we experience forgiveness, which leads to reconciliation. The more we experience forgiveness, the more free we are to love. The more we choose the way of forgiveness, the more we open ourselves to experiencing intimacy and closeness.

Anger does not have to destroy marriage. As we encounter anger, *we have a choice.* Our choice is between the way of bitterness—which cancels out intimacy and leaves us isolated and alone; and the way of forgiveness—which opens the door to intimacy and love.

The process of anger can be pictured as on the following page.

What if you have, over the years, chosen the way of bitterness; what is the solution? Can you experience change? The answer is yes! The solution is still FORGIVENESS!

THE PROCESS OF ANGER

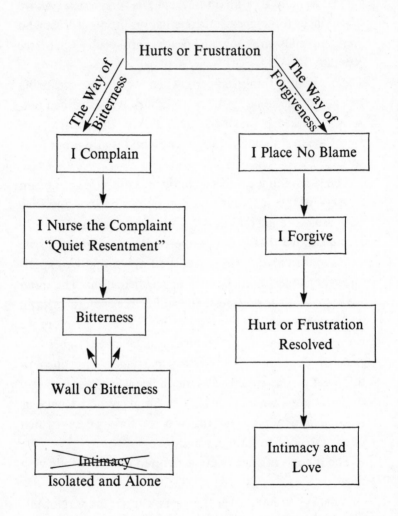

Because bitterness has been built up over years, the process of forgiveness may take some time as well. But that process begins with a commitment to one small step in the direction of forgiveness—of your partner as well as of yourself. Only forgiveness can cancel out the debts of the past.

QUESTIONS TO CONSIDER:

1. Think of a time when you have been able to experience forgiveness. Share your thoughts with your spouse.
2. What are some of the reasons why we find it so hard to forgive? Is it harder for you to forgive someone else, or to forgive yourself? Why?
3. Spend some time alone thinking of possible "roots of bitterness" that might be buried in the corner of the tent of your life. What would be a small first step you could take to begin to get rid of that bitterness? Could you share that step with your spouse?

Forgiveness is a journey of many steps. . . .

DAVID AUGSBURGER

9

A Commitment to
a Direction

"I forgive you, but I can't forget!" How many times have
we said that, or been on the receiving end of that statement, and later on wondered if the forgiveness was gen-
uine. Somehow we believe that if we forgive, we should
also forget. And after we tell someone we forgive him, we
are confused because we still are aware of feelings of hurt,
anger, and resentment. We feel that once we forgive, we
should be finished with it. We assume that forgiveness is a
one-step event.

David Augsburger, in his book *Caring Enough to Forgive,* says "Forgiveness, which is a complex and demanding process, is often reduced to a single act of accepting
another. In spite of the pain, hurt, loss and wrongdoing
that stand between us, we are encouraged to forgive in a
single act of resolving all by giving unconditional inclu-

133

sion. Such a step becomes too large for any human to take in a single bound. Forgiveness is a journey of many steps, each of which can be extremely difficult, all of which are to be taken carefully, thoughtfully, and with deep reflection."

Most of us resist the idea of forgiveness as a process. We want quick results—now! We want change. When we are faced with the need to change something in our lives, we usually think that we have to do it all at once, and we have to do it right the first time. No wonder we resist change.

A young couple was struggling with their commitment to each other, and to their marriage. The wife had moved out over the weekend and was trying to tell her husband how she felt. She was hurt and extremely frustrated. She explained to me that for years she had lived in constant fear of his temper. Even though he had never hurt her physically, he had on one occasion broken a door, and put several holes in the wall.

The previous Friday had been the last straw for her. He had been moody all week, and when she failed to respond properly to something he said at the dinner table, he came unglued. For four hours, he alternated from silent sulking to crying and shouting about all the things he thought were wrong with her. She had slept on the couch that night and hoped that Saturday would be different. When he started in on her again that morning, she grabbed some of her things and left. Their meeting in my office was the first time they had talked with each other since.

He had had several days to reflect and now was very apologetic about what had happened. But each time he

gave a reason for his moodiness, she reminded him of similar explosions in the past, finally ending up with the account of how he had broken a door and punched holes in
the wall.

With that he stood up and started pacing the floor,
pleading with her to forget the past. Over and over he said,
"Why can't you forget that? Why won't you ever forgive
me?" The more desperate he became the more silent she
became. When I asked her, "What makes it so difficult for
you to let go of those old events?" all she could say was, "I
just can't, that's all."

When he finally sat back down, he asked me, "Why
can't she commit herself to our marriage? If only she would
make that commitment, we'd have a great marriage!"
When I commented to her that she must be feeling a lot of
pressure from his statement, she agreed, and then added,
"He expects me to act like it never happened, and I can't!
How can I forget all the horrible things he said about me? I
just can't—it hurts too much to forget. Why can't he just
accept that I can't forget? He brings up things from the
past, too. He says he forgives me, but I hear about it later.
Isn't that the same thing?"

As we talked together, it became clear that each of them
expected the other person to do the forgiving and forget-
ting all at once. But neither one of them knew how. They
saw forgiveness as a one-time event and ended up paralyzed because forgiving seemed like too large a step to
take. They were overwhelmed by their fear that the same
things would happen again in the future if they let go of

the past. So they hung on to the past in an effort to protect themselves against their fears of the future. The result was that they had *nothing* in the present.

The way to break out of their paralyzed state was to focus more on the present. "What is it you wish you had in your marriage *today?*" I asked them both. As they tried to answer my question, it became clear to each of them that they wanted the same things. They wanted intimacy and closeness, love and understanding. Once they could state some positive things to focus on as their *present* desires in their marriage, we had a starting point for change. It was a small step, but it was a *step in the direction* of forgiveness. When I asked the wife if she could comfortably make a commitment to move in that direction, she replied, "Sure, I can do that."

One of the benefits of focusing on what *we want* in our marriage today, rather than focusing on what *we don't* want, is that it helps us see that change is worth the effort. We know that we want to experience certain things in our marriage relationship, but our tendency is to focus on what we want to eliminate. While we are seeking love and intimacy, we focus our attention on behaviors we want the other person to stop. We not only lose sight of what we desire, we also create all kinds of pressure on our partner. That pressure usually works in the opposite direction, pushing us even further away from what we want.

We need to return to the present by letting go of the past. We let go of the past more easily by seeing forgiveness as a "journey of many steps." And when we tell ourselves that we are only, at this time, going to make a commitment *to head in the direction* of the desired change, the pressure dissipates.

Often, we are well-meaning in our intentions and behaviors in our marriage, but either the pressures to change, or the paralysis of being stuck in the past, or fear of the future make us feel that we *can't* change. We can break out of that situation by taking the following steps in the direction of forgiveness.

STEP 1: *Visualize what you would like to experience in your marriage.* Use your imagination—anything is possible! What are you longing for in your relationship with your spouse? Don't evaluate your desires, simply try to see what positive things you long to experience together.

The couple we talked about earlier identified several abstract ideas, including love, intimacy, closeness, and understanding, which they wanted in their marriage. These are good concepts, but they needed to make them more concrete. So I asked them to imagine themselves in their relationship, experiencing all of these things—what kind of behaviors would be taking place. How would they act? What would a typical day be like?

They struggled with this one, but finally came up with these: We would be having fun together, going different places. We would be able to talk about our feelings without being defensive. We would share responsibility around the house, including housework, disciplining the kids, and doing special projects. She added that he would tell her about their finances, so she would know where they stood. He included in his visualization that when she got angry she would stick to the subject.

Once they had used their imagination to describe some of the positive behaviors that would be evidence that they were enjoying a loving, intimate, close relationship, they were ready for the next step.

STEP 2: *Define one small, specific, positive step you could take in the direction of your visualized relationship.* This step is difficult, but it is an essential step in the process of forgiveness. If we are ever going to reach our objectives in building the kind of relationship we desire, what would one of the first steps be?

The couple worked on this one between sessions and came up with some ideas that included taking one evening a week to have a "date night" and making a list of the things to be done around the house, and then agreeing to do one thing a week from the other person's list. They said they could take a course together at the junior college, on parenting, in order to learn more about how to raise their children.

We took all the ideas they listed and talked about which ones were either more appealing or more important. Then I explained again to them that what they were doing was making a commitment to a direction in their marriage. Since they were making that commitment, I asked them which item on their list would be a comfortable starting point for moving in the direction they had defined. They felt that they needed to have some fun together again, so they chose the "date night" idea.

It was very important that they understood they were *not* committing themselves to having a "date night" once a week. They were making a commitment to move in the direction of a more loving, close, intimate, and understanding relationship. As a part of their response to that commitment, they were only agreeing that a "date night" would be a comfortable first step to take in that direction.

If the couple felt they were making a commitment to having a "date night" once a week, it would become an end in itself. After a couple of dates, one of them might begin to feel reluctant to go. But if they can keep things in proper perspective—that the "date night" is a response to their commitment to move in the direction of a loving understanding relationship—then they might feel, after a couple of dates, that something else might be more helpful in moving them in the direction of their desired relationship. They might want to keep the "date night" and add something else, or drop it. Either way, it is not a failure, for their commitment is to a direction.

STEP 3: *Begin to act "as if" the other partner means well by what he or she does.* This step is an important ingredient in making a commitment to a direction work. Once the couple has decided on the specific, small, positive first step they are going to take, they each agree to act "as if" the other person is actively involved in the process, and to act "as if" the things he or she does and says are meant in a positive way.

One of the things that happens when we are paralyzed by anger or fear is that we tend to interpret everything the other person does in a bad light. If something is said that could be understood in two ways, we usually interpret it in the more negative way. This is especially true in a tense relationship.

Sometimes you simply have to *pretend* that the other person means well by what he or she says or does. I worked with a couple who had been married almost fifty years. Their relationship could hardly be called a marriage, for they had literally fought with each other from the first day they were married. Separately, they were enjoyable people, but when they were together, no one stayed around long. They had been to counseling before because her employer had required her to get counseling help in order to keep her job. Her temper made her a terror even at work.

Together we worked through many of the steps outlined in this book. They made half-hearted attempts, but nothing seemed to make any difference in their relationship. They were bitter, angry people, and they were firmly entrenched in the way of bitterness. Finally, I suggested this step—pretend your partner *means well* by anything he or she says or does. They agreed. She even seemed positive about what might happen.

Two weeks later, they said they had just enjoyed the best two weeks in their marriage. I asked them to tell me how they "pretended." He said that whenever she would start shouting at the TV, he pretended she wasn't mad at him, she was just getting involved in what she was watching.

She told me that whenever he got quiet and moody around the house, she pretended he was tired from work, and that he wasn't rejecting her. They told me about other situations when they did the same thing, and how good they were starting to feel about each other. I didn't tell them that what they were pretending—that the other person meant well—was probably true and in most situations had been true over the years as well.

STEP 4: *As you begin to feel better about each other, add another small, new, desired behavior to the process.* In response to your commitment to a direction, you have agreed on a small beginning step. Remember, that new behavior is not an end in itself but is only a step in the direction of your commitment. So is the new behavior you add to the first one.

When the "date night" becomes a comfortable, fun experience for our first couple, they will agree to add another item from their list as the next step in the process. Because they are enjoying each other, and feeling a little more comfortable about the relationship, they may decide to take a class together on parenting. Or they may decide on something completely different that wasn't even on their original list.

The second couple begins to feel better about each other because they are breaking some old relational patterns of behavior that have been tearing away at the foundation of their marriage. When they begin to feel that they no longer need to pretend, it will be a good time to add another small, positive behavior to their process. Each new behavior is a step taken in response to their commitment to a direction.

The amazing thing that happens when we begin to move together in the right direction is that, even though we never forget, we begin to remember less. At that point we begin to understand forgiveness as a process—as a life-style. Each step in the process makes the next step a little easier, for the process of forgiveness is self-rewarding. Healthy, growing marriages are built around a life-style of forgiveness. Any couple can commit themselves to that direction.

QUESTIONS TO CONSIDER:

1. Think about what would happen if you were to pretend for a whole week that everything your partner did was "meant well." Try it for seven days and don't tell your partner what you are doing until after you have done it.
2. Visualize some of the things you would like to be enjoying in your marriage today. Share these with your partner.
3. Define one small, specific, positive step you can take in response to your commitment to the direction of what you desire in your marriage. Share it with your partner.

Now your attitudes and thoughts must all be constantly changing for the better.

EPHESIANS 4:23 TLB

Epilogue

Refresh *Your* Marriage

In this book, we have focused on the emotion of anger. Whether it is suppressed, repressed, or expressed, it is the major cause of problems in marriage today. Anger is the problem behind the other problems encountered in any close relationship. It is the emotion that blocks us in our search for love and intimacy.

As we have seen, the problem with anger is compounded by our difficulty in effectively communicating to the other person what we are angry about. When frustrated, we often stash the anger away, deep within ourselves. Medical research is showing that many of the physical problems we experience are the result of holding the emotions of anger and fear inside.

We also pointed out that the opposite response is equally destructive. If we express anger, or ventilate it, all we end up doing is accelerating the emotions we feel, causing them to increase or expand. Instead of being less angry, we end up more angry. The result is that in our search for closeness and intimacy within marriage, we find isolation instead. Our lack of knowledge of constructive patterns in defusing anger's intensity causes it to become a barrier that keeps us from reaching our goals in marriage.

But there is a solution! We pointed out that the key to effectively defusing anger lies within our Self-Talk—the way we think. Our thoughts create our emotions. If we feel anger, it is because, in our thoughts, we are making demands. These demands are irrational, usually because they are demands that the past be different. No one can change the past, but our irrational thinking makes us attempt to do the impossible. We can resolve our anger by changing our demands and expectations into wishes, wants, and desires. We break through the barrier of anger when we learn to communicate effectively by using the language of desires instead of the language of demands.

When anger becomes bitterness, the process of working on our Self-Talk may seem inadequate. Resentments and bitterness are difficult to break through. Sometimes the hurts are so deep that we feel that we don't even want to try to process them. But the solution to resentment and bitterness is found in forgiveness. A life-style of forgiveness will destroy the roots of bitterness nurtured over the years.

We have covered the areas of resolving daily anger and uprooting the long-term resentments and bitterness—all barriers to love, closeness, understanding and intimacy.

Healthy, growing marriages are nurtured when we communicate our anger effectively in an atmosphere of forgiveness.

Another way of summarizing what we have been saying
is to conceptualize the principles for resolving anger by
seeing the word FORGIVE in the following way:

F—FOCUS on our responsibility in the situation.

Our natural tendency is to focus on what the other person did or did not do. We think that if we can just educate
our partner so that he can see the "error of his way," angry
situations would be resolved. Usually both people are trying to do the same thing. The result is that no one takes responsibility for his or her own behavior in a situation.

Think what would happen if the next time you and your
mate have a disagreement, you focus your attention on
what *you* did or did not do during the events leading up to
the argument. In other words, take responsibility for your
behavior. If both partners do this, the argument won't last
very long.

O—ORIENT ourselves to the other person's point of view.

Not only do we take responsibility for our part in the
problem, but we go a step further and attempt to see the
situation from the viewpoint of our spouse. What was she
thinking? How might she have been perceiving the situation in question?

At first it may seem as if you are just guessing, but the
more you practice it the more proficient you will become in

seeing the problem from your mate's point of view. This takes some effort, for it means that in a tense situation, you attempt to put yourself in the other person's shoes and see life through his eyes.

R—RECOGNIZE that no one is totally to blame.

The tendency to blame someone else places us in a win-lose situation. The problem with win-lose attitudes is that in a marriage, no one wins when one partner wins—in reality both lose.

Whenever couples get into arguments over who caused the conflict, both people become defensive. The argument will move back and forth, from one person to the other, as each one seeks to win the argument by making the other person lose. What we don't realize is that if we make our partner lose, then we lose also. The only way we can really win is to help our spouse win. The only way either of us can end up winning is if both of us win. That means we cannot argue about who is to blame.

G—GIVE UP our expectations and demands.

Why do we persist in making demands when we don't have the ability to enforce them? All we end up doing is making ourselves angry. Yet how hard we fight to hold on to our "shoulds"! Perhaps the irrationality of making demands is best seen in the husband whose wife has just said she doesn't love him anymore. The more he demands that, as his wife, she must still love him, the less likely she will be able to love him. The only way she will ever be able to feel any love for him again is if he gives up his demand—if he gives her the right not to love him.

This is one of the paradoxes of life. Jesus showed us this when He said, "For whoever would save his life will lose it, and whoever loses his life for my sake will find it" (Matthew 16:25). Give up in order to receive. Give up your demands and expectations in order to gain what your heart desires and longs for in your marriage. It's risky, but when you attempt to enforce demands, you will usually end up losing what you desire.

I—IDENTIFY wants and desires.

Often we are afraid of this step; if we really say what it is we want or desire from our marriage, we may get turned down. That may be how it feels, but the results are usually the opposite. Whenever we risk sharing what we really long for in our marriage relationship, we usually find out that our partner is seeking the same thing.

But the important part of this principle is to communicate these wants and desires after we have identified them. What are the positive qualities we long for in our marriage? Talk about those in the language of wishes, wants, and desires. Change your thoughts to reflect that language of wishes, wants, and desires. The more you practice this form of Self-Talk, the less you will experience irrational feelings of anger.

V—VISUALIZE wants and desires "as if" accomplished.

Once we identify and are communicating our wants and

desires, we can use our imagination to visualize them as "already accomplished." All too often, we tend to minimize the power of our imagination. God has created us so that our mind is the control center of our life. That is why the Apostle Paul is so insistent on our renewing our minds. He tells us "whatever is true, whatever is honorable, whatever is just, whatever is pure, whatever is lovely, whatever is gracious, if there is any excellence, if there is anything worthy of praise, think about these things" (Philippians 4:8). "As a man thinks in his heart, so is he" (*see* Proverbs 23:7).

When we visualize, we are programming our minds and in turn our behavior as well.

E—EXPRESS our commitment to a direction by taking steps in that direction.

We need to say it out loud. We need to talk to our partners and tell them what we want in our marriage relationship, and then together make a commitment to begin taking steps in that direction. Commitment begins with making one small baby step, and then another, and then another. The commitment is to a direction—to a process. It is movement toward a goal, not a goal in and of itself. This is an exciting principle. We have seen couples who were stuck with hurts and fears break out of that stuck spot and start again on the path of togetherness and intimacy simply by committing themselves to move in that direction.

Sometimes reading books about marriage isn't enough. We may need the help of an objective third person—a marriage "helper." Some couples are reluctant to seek help, thinking that they should be able to fix things themselves. But if improvement doesn't occur, do something about it before the issues become so complex that you feel it is too late. Don't settle for less than you can have in marriage.

Other couples believe in preventive maintenance. They see a marriage therapist every so often, much like seeing their family doctor for their annual physical checkup. Some of the most rewarding things I see happening in marriage is with the couples who come to see me for a couple of sessions once or twice a year. They might say, "We're really doing fine with each other, but there are a few things happening that we wanted to check out with you." That's exciting! They're going to make it.

We believe that marriages can be healed. They can be vibrant, growing, living relationships. The longer a couple lives together, the more exciting the challenges and the richer the rewards. Our desire is that this book will add to both the challenges and the rewards in your marriage.